Classics of
Vegetable Cooking

# Tomatoes

**DUMONT**
**monte**

**Concept and execution:** Meidenbauer • Martin
Verlagsbüro, Munich
**Text and recipes:** Anna Thal, Dagmar Fronius-Gaier
**Editorial:** Matthias Edbauer, Susanne Maß,
Simone Steger
**Layout and typesetting:** Hubert Grafik Design, Munich
**Photography:** Brigitte Sporrer, Alena Hrbkova
**Food styling:** Hans Gerlach
**Cover design:** BOROS, Wuppertal
**© cover photograph:** Christel Rosenfeld
**Printing:** Druckerei Appl, Wemding
**Binding:** Sigloch, Künzelsau

© 2001 DuMont Buchverlag, Köln
DuMont monte, UK, London
All rights reserved

ISBN 3-7701-7045-8

Printed in Germany

## General hints

*Eggs:* If not otherwise stated, the eggs used in these recipes are of medium size. Eggs should not be eaten raw, particularly by babies, toddlers, pregnant women and old people, and it is strongly advised that any dish using raw eggs should be eaten immediately.

*Milk:* If not otherwise stated, milk used in these recipes is whole milk (3.5% fat content).

*Poultry:* Poultry should always be cooked right through before eating. You can tell if it is done by piercing it with a skewer. If the juices run out pink, then it is not ready and must be cooked for a longer time. If the juices are clear then the bird is done.

*Nuts:* Some of these recipes contain nuts or nut oil. People who have allergies or who tend to be allergic should avoid eating these dishes.

*Herbs:* If not otherwise stated, these recipes call for fresh herbs. If you cannot obtain these, the amounts in the recipes can be replaced with half the quantity of dried herbs.

*Alcohol:* Some of the recipes in this book contain alcohol. These dishes should not be served to children or sufferers from alcoholism.

The temperatures and times in these recipes are based on using a conventional oven. If you are using a fan oven, please follow the manufacturer's instructions .

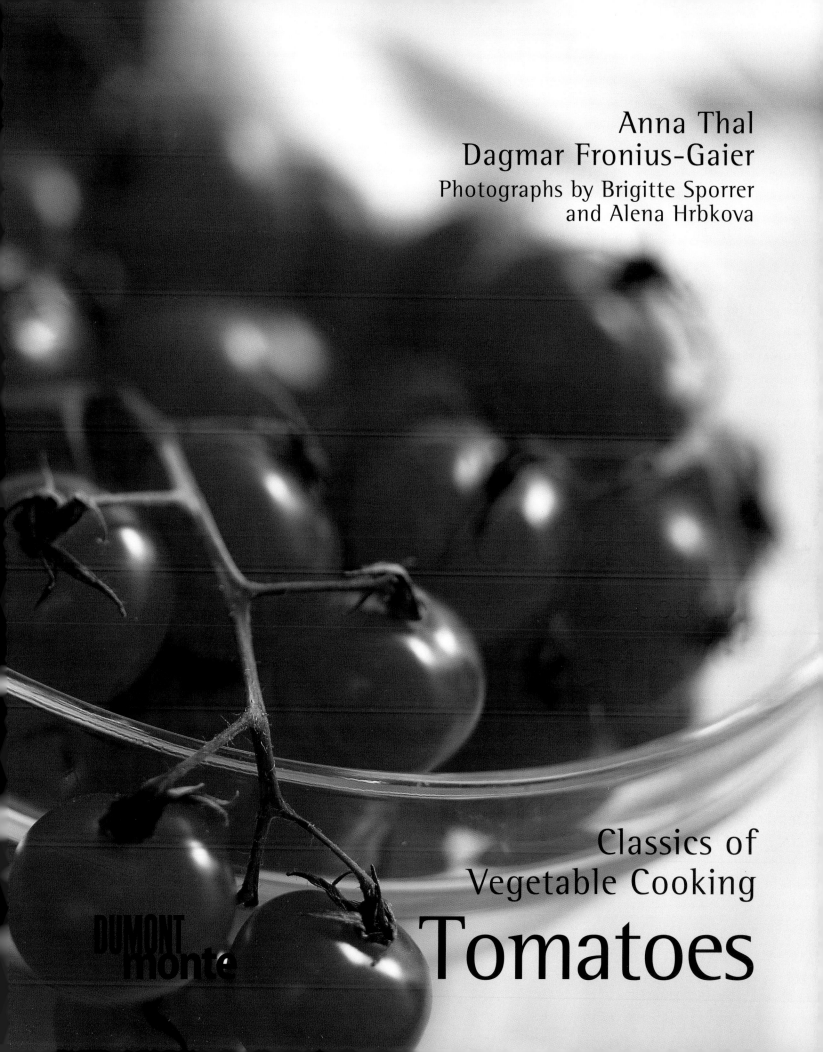

Anna Thal
Dagmar Fronius-Gaier
Photographs by Brigitte Sporrer
and Alena Hrbkova

Classics of
Vegetable Cooking
# Tomatoes

DuMONT monte

# Contents

# Introduction

The tomato is a round, juicy red fruit that is delicious whether eaten hot or cold, and it is a perfect accompaniment to almost any dish. It is undoubtedly one of the most versatile ingredients, appearing in salads, soups, starters (appetizers), main dishes, soufflés and snacks, as well as being a vegetable in its own right. It has a slightly sharp, acid taste with a touch of sweetness. It is used in almost every cuisine in the world and has been integrated into the national and regional dishes of many countries. So it is not surprising that the tomato should be used in even the most exotic dishes, and this book contains tomato recipes from all over the world. The tomato is actually a native of South America, where it originated in Peru.

## When the tomato was still called tomatl...

The story of the tomato began with the Incas and Aztecs who were the first to cultivate it. It was in the 16th century that Spanish explorers first came across the *tomatl* (which means "swollen fruits" in Aztec ), and brought its seeds back to Spain. But the tomato did not become part of European cuisine for another two centuries. At first it was believed to be a poisonous plant, and it was cultivated solely as an ornamental plant as late as the 18th century. The tomato met with a similar reception in the United States, and it was only in the 19th century that the tomato rose from its long sleep. Creole immigrants in South America were very fond of using it as a vegetable, especially with seafood.

Since then, the tomato has not stopped growing in popularity. By the end of the 19th century tomatoes were cultivated in many gardens in the southern states of the United States.

In Europe, this "love apple", "apple of paradise " or "golden apple", as the tomato was variously named, had a more difficult time to start with. Because the tomato was said to have aphrodisiac powers, the church intervened and succeeded in forbidding its consumption for a while. However, it was ultimately unable to stop its triumphant progress in European cuisine. Its great versatility was soon reflected in its many uses as a vegetable, purée or sauce, and the tomato became a popular ingredient in national cuisines in every part the world.

## The tomato becomes an international food

The tomato has been incorporated into dishes of many national cuisines. In Italy, tomatoes are used in sauces to accompany to pasta dishes (such as *spaghetti alla napoletana*), as a topping (on *bruschetta*), and in tomato salad (*insalata di pomodori*); in Spain, the tomato is the basic ingredient of the cold soup *gazpacho*, and in Greece it is used to make a country salad. In India, tomatoes are often used in combination with chickpeas and other vegetables, while TexMex cuisine is famous for its spicy tomato-based sauces seasoned with chilli pepper.

But tomatoes are not only used as a vegetable, in sauces and in soup. As tomato ketchup, it has become universally popular, and Henry J. Heinz's invention has become an omnipresent sauce on tables everywhere in the world. Americans enjoy ketchup with chips and hamburgers; in Asia ketchup is eaten with seafood, especially deep-fried shrimps, and in Thailand it is eaten with potato crisps. In Sweden it is poured onto pasta, while in Great-Britain it is eaten with fish and chips. In Spain, it is popular with omelettes.

## The tomato plant

Like the potato, the tomato belongs to the *Solanaceae* family. It does not need any daylight to flower. The stems and leaves of the tomato plant are covered with thin hairs, and it is these that give off the well-known, powerful tomato aroma when they are broken. The distinctive taste is the result of sugar and fruit acids. Because tomatoes need a mild climate, they are often cultivated in greenhouses in northern countries, while in warmer countries such as Spain, Italy, Greece, Turkey and Egypt, they are grown in the open.

## The colour of tomatoes

As the tomato ripens, the poisonous alkaloid solanine which is present in green tomatoes breaks down and disappears, while the new substances lycopin and carotin gradually develops. These are responsible for the tomato's red colour. The actual colour of the tomato depends on the fruit's degree of ripeness, which in turn depends on the light and warmth available. Besides the common red tomatoes there are also yellow, purple-black and green varieties. These particular green tomatoes are not unripe red ones but a particular tomato variety, *tomatillo*, which is native to Mexico and Central America.

## Tomato varieties

There is a wide range of tomato varieties, all varying in shape, taste and size. The tomato's size depends on the number of seed vessels it has; there are usually from two to ten. The beef tomato, for instance, has five or more seed vessels, while plum tomatoes have only two or three. Here are a few of the most popular tomato varieties:

### Tomatoes on the vine

Those tomatoes are harvested with the calyx and stem. This is only possible if all the fruit ripens at the same time.
*Use*: because of their very intense flavour these tomatoes are especially suitable for salads, as a raw snack or sandwich filling.

### Cherry tomatoes on the vine

These little round tomatoes are picked as large bunches and have a very intense, sweet flavour.
*Use*: as cherry tomatoes.

### Canned tomatoes

The kind of tomatoes used for canning are usually plum tomatoes because of their fruity aroma and the small quantity of seeds they contain. Peeled and chopped, preserved in their own juice, they are a simple, tasty alternative to fresh tomatoes in the preparation of many dishes.
*Use*: canned tomatoes are ideal for making tomato based sauces, soups and stews – especially when one is in a hurry.

### Plum tomatoes

These oval-shaped tomatoes are particularly popular because of their intense flavour.
*Use*: plum tomatoes are ideal for dishes where the tomato flavour is intended to be dominant, such as in salads, sauces or soups.

### Beef tomatoes

As the name suggest, this variety is particularly fleshy. The most striking features of this variety are the many ribs, the small number of seeds and the weight of each individual tomato. Indeed, some can weigh as much as 1 kg (over 2 lb).
*Use*: these sweet-sour tomatoes can be hollowed out and stuffed with vegetables, meat or fish, then baked. Because they are very firm, they are ideal for soufflés, savoury puddings and sandwich filling.

### Cherry or cocktail tomatoes

These little round tomatoes have a very delicate flavour and add a pleasant decorative touch to hot dishes and cold platters.
*Use*: whole to garnish salads, or in pasta sauces.

### Red round tomatoes

This is the best known and commonest variety, and is found in various sizes. The seed vessels contain a large number of yellow-green seeds, embedded in a jelly-like fruit juice.
*Use*: raw, in sauces and in soups; when used in salads, the seeds should be removed because the salad would otherwise become too wet.

### Sardinian

This variety of tomato, a native to Sardinia as its name suggests, is of small to medium size, very firm and particularly aromatic.
*Use*: in salads or in the classic Italian starter (appetizer) tomatoes with mozzarella and basil, in which the firmness and intense flavour of the Sardinian tomato is at its best.

### Tamarillo

The tree tomato is a cultivated wild variety native to the high plateaus of Peru, Ecuador and Columbia. It is now available in many supermarkets, in the autumn and winter season. The intensely dark red colour of the skin makes this variety particularly attractive. When sliced, the Tamarillo tomato reveals orange-coloured flesh and seeds that are almost black. Their flavour is also very unusual, perhaps best described as bitter, sweet and sour.
*Use*: it adds a very special touch to salads, sauces, puddings and jams (preserves).

## Green tomatoes

What are these true green tomatoes? They are a wild variety of the tomato called *tomatillo*, native to Mexico, with the unusual characteristic that they do not turn red when they ripen. They are extremely hard to obtain in Europe. European cuisine therefore has to make use of green tomatoes, in other words, red tomatoes which are not yet ripe .
However, it should be remembered that unripe tomatoes which are still green contain large amounts of solanine. Because of its indigestibility, solanine should only be consumed in very small quantities. On

the other hand, red tomatoes which are fully ripe are completely safe because the solanine is gradually broken down as the tomato develops and ripens. Even yellow-green tomatoes contain much less solanine, as confirmed by the following figures: 100 g/3½ oz of hard, green tomatoes contain 9 to 32 mg solanine, and pale green tomatoes 7 to 13 mg, while half-ripe, orange tomatoes contain between 0.1 to 1.8 mg. A solanine content of less than 20 mg per 100 g/3½ oz fresh tomatoes is absolutely harmless to humans. People who like green tomatoes can therefore safely try some of the green tomato recipes in this book.

Green tomato jam (preserve) is available in the shops and tomatoes preserved in lactic acid are perfectly safe to eat. If you make your own green tomato jam (preserve), the addition of sugar will reduce the solanine levels by 35%. The same happens when tomatoes are bottled in lactic acid.

## Buying tomatoes and storage

To get the best value and greatest enjoyment from tomatoes, buy firm red tomatoes without any pressure marks. Only then will the tomatoes be able to develop their full flavour. If green tomatoes are bought to be stored, the reality is that they will never achieve their full flavour, even when fully ripened.

Here are a few simple tips for storing tomatoes which will make them last longer:

- Remove the tomatoes from their packaging immediately after purchase.
- Store them in a well-ventilated cool, dry place.
- The ideal storage temperature is between 10° and 13°C (50° and 55°F).
- Tomatoes should not be stored in a refrigerator because they will lose some of their flavour.

Be careful not to store cucumbers and tomatoes together. Tomatoes release the natural gas ethylene which turns cucumbers yellow and make them go soft.

When preparing tomatoes for salads, soups etc., remove the stipules and stalk as well as all the green parts because they contain solanine. Tomatoes are more digestible if they are peeled before cooking. This is because the skin remains tough even when cooked. Peeling tomatoes is easier if the skin is first cut crossways with a knife, and the tomatoes are then blanched in boiling water. The skin rolls up where it has been cut so that it can easily be peeled off.

## Vitamins, minerals and nutritional value

Average quantities per 100 g/3½ oz fresh tomatoes (edible parts only):

### Vitamins

| | |
|---|---|
| B1 | 0.06 mg |
| B2 | 0.04 mg |
| B6 | 0.10 mg |
| Biotin | 4.0 µg |
| C | 24.54 mg |
| E | 0.81 mg |
| Folic acid | 39.00 µg |
| K | 9.00 µg |

### Minerals

| | |
|---|---|
| Chlorine | 60 mg |
| Iron | 0.50 mg |
| Fluoride | 24.00 µg |
| Iodine | 1.70 µg |
| Potassium | 242 mg |
| Calcium | 14 mg |
| Copper | 60.00 µg |
| Magnesium | 13 mg |
| Manganese | 140.00 µg |
| Sodium | 6.0 mg |
| Phosphorus | 26.00 mg |
| Zinc | 0.17 mg |

### Nutrients/Nutritional value

| | |
|---|---|
| Protein | 0.95 g |
| Fat | 0.21 g |
| Glucose | 1.11 g |
| Carbohydrate | 2.60 g |
| kcal | 17.00 |
| Kilojoule | 73 |

## Healthy cooking

In studying at the large number of minerals and vitamins contained in tomatoes, the high level of potassium is striking. The presence of other minerals including copper, zinc, phosphorus, calcium, iron and magnesium makes the tomato a particularly healthy fruit which plays an important part in the diet. Apart from its vitamin and mineral content, the tomato has other health-related properties. It is very low in calories, it acts as a diuretic, it helps reduce blood-pressure and it has a beneficial effect on the heart and kidneys. It also alleviates rheumatism, gout, arthritis and problems of circulation.

The most remarkable property of the tomato is its pigment lycopin which is responsible for the tomato's red colour. What is very unusual about this substance is its stability when heated, which means that the tomato maintains its health-promoting qualities, whether prepared as ketchup, used in a sauce or served as a soup. This makes tomatoes a valuable, healthy addition to the daily diet.

This delicious red fruit has other beneficial medicinal properties. It stimulates the appetite, reduces stress, has a positive effect on the psyche and helps combat insomnia. The tomato even has cosmetic properties: it is an excellent remedy for open pores. Freshly cut slices of tomatoes are applied where needed; after leaving them for a few minutes, the pores will begin to close.

## Home-grown tomatoes

People who want to enjoy the pleasures of home-grown tomatoes do not need to have a garden of their own. A balcony or terrace will be quite sufficient to accommodate a few tomato plants such as balcony -, pot – or espalier tomatoes.

Tomato plants can be grown in pots at room temperature or in a greenhouse from the second half of March onwards. The young plants should not be planted outside before all danger of frost is past.

The young tomato plants require a warm situation, sheltered from the elements. They should be planted at intervals of at least 50 cm/20 in from each other. A supporting cane should be provided for each plant, which the tomato will need as it develops. This support is inserted directly into the soil next to the plant. As the tomato plant grows, it should be tied to this support.

## Watering and fertilizing

Growing tomatoes is not an expensive or difficult activity. The most important requirement is that they should be watered regularly and generously – but do not let the plants sit in water! To avoid the notorious tomato blight, care should be taken not to spray the leaves of the tomato plant when watering. Also, it is advisable to remove the bottom leaves; this will help

protect the plants from mould and rot. However, the remaining leaves are very important to shade the ripening tomatoes.

In summer, the tomato plants should be given a liquid compound fertilizer at regular intervals. The following tips will ensure a good crop of tomatoes:

With the exception of bush tomatoes, always remove all side branches of each tomato plant. This allows the plant to concentrate all its power in the development of fruit. Always use your fingers to remove the side branches. rather than a knife which could spread bacteria. The leaves of the tomato plant which you have removed in pruning can also be used as fertilizer. But only healthy leaves should be used for this purpose.

If in the autumn it becomes necessary to harvest tomatoes that are not yet fully ripe because of the danger of frost, these can be stored for a long time in a box loosely filled with garden peat. But make sure that the tomatoes do not touch each other.

# Snacks and salads

Snacks and salads make excellent starters (appetizers) but they can also be meals in their own right if the amounts of the various ingredients are increased. The great versatility of the tomato and the many ways in which it can be prepared give a wide variety of possibilities. There is something for every taste and every occasion, ranging all the way from the savoury, such as Mozzarella parcels with bacon and tomatoes (page 23), to the sweet (Honey tomatoes baked in the oven, page 24).

# Bruschetta

The supreme light Italian snack: slices of white bread, toasted, topped with diced tomatoes and seasoned with herbs. Served before the starter (appetizer), it sharpens the appetite. It is also a delicious accompaniment to an Italian country wine, such as Montepulciano d'Abruzzo.

4 medium tomatoes
½ bunch basil
½ bunch parsley
1 clove garlic
salt
pepper
8 slices white bread
4 tablespoons olive oil

❶ Cut the tomatoes into quarters and remove the seeds. Dice the tomato quarters. Coarsely chop the basil and parsley. Peel and chop the cloves of garlic.

❷ Mix the herbs and diced tomatoes in a bowl, add the chopped garlic and season with salt and pepper.

❸ Toast some slices of white bread and sprinkle with olive oil. Put some of the tomato mixture on each slice of toast. Serve immediately.

**Serves 4. About 294 kcal per serving**

# Green tomatoes with cucumbers

This recipe is ideal for anyone who stands in their vegetable garden in the autumn and wonders what to do with all the green tomatoes which refuse to turn red.

6 large green tomatoes (already showing some traces of orange)
1 cucumber
butter and oil for frying
1–2 cups condensed milk
1–2 cups fine porridge (rolled) oats
salt
pepper

❶ Pre-heat the oven at its lowest setting, 80°C (175°F). Cover a baking sheet with kitchen paper.

❷ Cut the tomatoes and peeled cucumber into slices 1 cm/⅜ in thick.

❸ Heat equal amounts of butter and oil in a large frying pan

❹ Dip the tomato and cucumber slices in condensed milk and coat on both sides with rolled oats. Carefully fry a few at a time on both sides until the vegetables begin to turn brown.

❺ Place the fried tomatoes and cucumbers on the baking sheet and put in the oven to keep warm. Season with salt and pepper before serving.

**Serves 4. About 225 kcal per serving**

# Unleavened bread with tomatoes and yoghurt

800 g/1¾ lb ripe sweet tomatoes

2 red onions

1 bunch smooth parsley

500 ml/17 fl oz (2¼ cups) yoghurt

sugar

salt

cayenne pepper

paprika

1 tablespoon lemon juice

1 loaf unleavened (matzo) bread

An interesting vegetarian dish which should be served on a plate and eaten with a knife and fork; this is the best way to enjoy the refreshing yoghurt sauce which combines so well with the bread.

❶ Cut the tomatoes into small cubes and slice the peeled onions wafer-thin. Coarsely chop the parsley.

❷ Put the yoghurt in a bowl and stir vigorously with a whisk until smooth. Mix together the diced tomatoes, onion rings, parsley, sugar and seasoning. Add lemon juice to taste.

❸ Cut the unleavened bread into 8 slices and cut in half horizontally. Place the bread slices on four plates and cover with the tomato and yoghurt mixture.

**Serves 4. About 131 kcal per serving**

# Parmesan and tomato muffins

130 g/5 oz (1¼ cups) flour

75 g/3 oz (9 tablespoons) maize flour

2 teaspoons baking powder

½ teaspoon salt

150 g/5 oz (1½ cups) freshly grated Parmesan

1 egg, room temperature

60 ml/3 fl oz (6 tablespoons) oil

250 ml/8 fl oz (1 cup) milk

oil for the moulds

8–10 cherry tomatoes

50 g/2 oz rocket

Quick and easy to prepare, this is a party hit which looks very decorative on a cold buffet table. The Parmesan may be replaced by freshly grated Pecorino, an Italian hard cheese made from sheep's milk.

❶ Pre-heat the oven to 180°C (350°F), Gas mark 4. Mix the flour, cornflour (starch), baking powder, salt and Parmesan in a bowl. Stir in the egg, oil and milk.

❷ Grease the hollows of a muffin tin with oil and fill with the dough. Bake for about 20 minutes in the pre-heated oven. Remove the muffins from the mould and leave to cool on a cake rack.

❸ Cut the cherry tomatoes into slices. Cut the muffins in half horizontally. Cover with the sliced tomato and rocket and serve at once.

**Serves 4. About 550 kcal per serving**

# Tomato bread-pudding

A pudding need not necessarily be seen as a chocolate, strawberry or vanilla dessert, served at the end of the meal. It can also be made from bread and tomatoes, and served as a starter (appetizer) – simply delicious!

8 slices white bread

2 large cans chopped tomatoes, (800 g/1¾ lb each)

3 tablespoons brown sugar

2 teaspoons sweet soya sauce

a few drops of Tabasco

salt

1 tablespoon cream

50 g/2 oz (4 tablespoons) butter

❶ Remove the crusts from the white bread, and cut the crust and bread slices into cubes.

❷ Put the chopped tomatoes with their juice in a pan and add the brown sugar, soya sauce, tabasco and a pinch of salt. Bring to the boil. Simmer for about 5 minutes, stirring continuously. Stir in the cream; check the seasoning and adjust to taste.

❸ Pre-heat the oven to 220°C (425°F), Gas mark 7.

❹ Melt the butter in a pan. Put the cubes of white bread in a bowl and pour the melted butter over them. Stir until the bread cubes have absorbed all the melted butter. Put the bread cubes into four ramekins and pour the tomato mixture on top.

❺ Bake the tomato bread-pudding in the middle of the oven for about 20 minutes. Remove from the oven and serve hot in the ramekins.

**Serves 4. About 364 kcal per serving**

# Mozzarella parcels with bacon and tomatoes

The combination of mozzarella and tomatoes is always a successful one: the mild, slightly sharp taste of this cow's milk cheese complements and emphasizes the sweet flavour of the tomatoes.

**1** Let the mozzarella and sun-dried tomatoes drain thoroughly on kitchen paper. Chop the shallots and tomatoes finely. Cut each piece of mozzarella in half horizontally.

**2** Pre-heat the oven to its highest setting, 250°C (480°F).

**3** Cover each half piece of mozzarella with some chopped shallots and tomatoes. Sprinkle with basil and cover with the other half piece of mozzarella. Wrap each mozzarella parcel with a slice of streaky bacon.

**4** Pour some basil oil into an ovenproof dish and put the mozzarella parcels in it next to each other. Put under the grill for about 5 minutes.

**5** Just before serving, sprinkle the mozzarella parcels with basil oil and add some white pepper.

**Serves 4. About 630 kcal per serving**

**4 packs mozzarella
(200 g/7 oz each)**

**50 g/2 oz dried tomatoes**

**2 shallots**

**1 teaspoon dried basil**

**4 thin slices streaky bacon**

**3 tablespoons basil-infused oil**

**white pepper**

# Baked
# Parmesan tomatoes

Easy to prepare and quick to make, these baked tomatoes topped with Parmesan are delicious with buttered slices of white bread.

oil for the baking sheet

8 beef tomatoes

40 g/1½ oz (3 tablespoons) herb butter

25 g/1 oz (¼ cup) grated Parmesan

❶ Pre-heat the oven to 200°C (400°F), Gas mark 6. Grease a baking sheet generously with oil.

❷ Using a knife, make a cross-shaped incision 0.5 cm/under ¼ in deep in the base of the tomato (the opposite end to the stalk). Put the tomatoes next to each other on the baking sheet and bake in the oven for about 15 minutes.

❸ Remove the tomatoes from the oven and put a teaspoon of herb butter on the incision of each of the tomatoes. Grate some Parmesan and sprinkle on top of the tomatoes. Now put the tomatoes, topped with Parmesan under a very hot grill for about 5 minutes.

**For 4 people, per serving about 212 kcal.**

# Baked
# honey tomatoes

A sweet temptation. The honey brings out the tomato's own sweet flavour while the tarragon, salt and pepper add a spicy note to the dish.

butter for the baking dish

8 large ripe tomatoes

4 tablespoons breadcrumbs

2 teaspoons salt

2 teaspoons white pepper

1 teaspoon tarragon

4 tablespoons honey

40 g/1½ oz (3 tablespoons) butter

❶ Pre-heat the oven to 200°C (400°F), Gas mark 6. Generously butter a large oven-proof dish.

❷ Cut the top off each tomato at the end opposite the stalk to open up the seed vessels; reserve the "lids". Put the tomatoes on some kitchen paper with the cut end downward so that the seeds and juices run out. Carefully remove the remaining seeds with the tip of a knife. Put the tomatoes stalk end downwards in the oven-proof dish.

❸ Add salt, pepper and tarragon to the breadcrumbs and mix well. Put the honey in the tomatoes and add the breadcrumb mixture on top. Put a teaspoon of butter on each tomato and put the lid back on.

❹ Bake the honey tomatoes in the oven for about 20 minutes. Then put under the oven grill at maximum temperature for about 5 minutes. Serve hot.

**Serves 4. About 210 kcal per serving**

# Courgette (zucchini) mousse with tomato salad

It is true that this delicious courgette (zucchini) mousse takes time to prepare but the result is definitely worth it. This exquisite dish is a pleasure to the eye as well as to the palate and therefore makes an ideal party starter (appetizer).

2 large courgettes (zucchini)

salt

300 ml/10 fl oz (1¼ cups) vegetable stock (broth)

150 g/5 oz coarse porridge (rolled) oats

8 sheets white gelatine

400 g/14 oz curd cheese

2 tablespoons wine vinegar

1 bunch chives

2 egg white

125 ml/4 fl oz (½ cup) cream

300 g/10 oz tomatoes

100 g/3½ oz mushrooms

1 shallot

2 tablespoons balsamic vinegar

sugar

pepper

4 tablespoons vegetable oil

❶ Peel the courgettes (zucchini) and cut into small cubes. Sprinkle with salt and put to one side.

❷ Put the vegetable stock (broth) in a saucepan and bring to the boil. Add the porridge (rolled) oats and simmer on a very low flame for 30 minutes. Then pour the vegetable stock (broth) through a sieve and reserve the liquid. Put the porridge (rolled) oats to one side.

❸ Soften the gelatine in cold water. When ready, take the gelatine out the water and squeeze well. Heat the vegetable stock (broth) again and dissolve the gelatine in it.

❹ Put the curd cheese in a large bowl and stir until smooth. Add the vegetable stock (broth), cooled but not yet set, to the curd cheese and stir well to obtain a smooth mixture. Then add the cubed courgettes (zucchini), porridge (rolled) oats, wine vinegar and half the chopped chives to the curd cheese and vegetable stock (broth) mixture. Stir well. Now beat the egg whites and cream separately until stiff. Fold carefully into the curd cheese and vegetable stock (broth) mixture.

❺ Rinse six cups in cold water and fill with the courgette (zucchini) mousse. Put in the refrigerator for about 2 hours to set.

❻ For the salad, clean and slice the mushrooms, slice the tomatoes and chop the shallots finely.

❼ Make a salad dressing with balsamic vinegar, sugar, pepper, salt and vegetable oil. Add the chopped shallots. Divide the tomato and mushroom salad into portions on separate plates, then pour the dressing over. Sprinkle the remaining chives on the salad. Remove the mousse from the cups and put in the centre of each plate, arranging the salad around it.

**Serves 6. About 468 kcal per serving**

# Ciabatta with leaf spinach and tomato filling

Ciabatta is a particularly crusty type of Italian white bread. This delicious leaf spinach and tomato filling is also very good on a baguette.

**❶** Peel the shallots, cut into small cubes and sweat in some oil until transparent. Peel the garlic, press it and add to the shallots. Add the frozen spinach and cook gently for about 15 minutes. Season with salt, pepper and nutmeg.

**❷** Pre-heat the oven to 200°C (400°F), Gas mark 6.

**❸** Cut the tomatoes and Camembert into slices. Cut the ciabatta in half and cut each half open. Spread a thin layer of herb butter on the bottom half of each piece of ciabatta and arrange the tomato slices on top. Spoon the spinach mixture on top and cover with slices of camembert.

**❹** Place the pieces of ciabatta covered with tomato, spinach and camembert on a baking sheet and put in the oven to brown for a maximum of 10 minutes. After about 5 minutes, put the halves without topping in the oven as well.

**❺** Take the ciabatta with leaf-spinach and tomato topping and serve hot. The other halves can either be put next to each piece or on top.

**Serves 4. About 491 kcal per serving**

2 shallots

1 tablespoon oil

1 clove garlic

450 g/1 lb leaf spinach, frozen

salt

white pepper

nutmeg

250 g/9 oz soft Camembert

600 g/1¼ lb tomatoes

2 ciabatta (about 250 g/9 oz each)

50 g/2 oz (4 tablespoons) herb butter

# Tomatoes
# with herb sauce

Tofu (bean curd) has been an important protein source in the daily diet of the people of China and Japan for over 2000 years, and it is used in many dishes. Made from soya bean milk, it is low in calories, easy to digest and very versatile. For instance, it can be roasted, baked or fried. Smoked tofu (bean curd) has pleasant lightly smoked aroma. It is available in health food shops and supermarkets with a good health food section.

**6 small, firm tomatoes**

**1 courgette (zucchini)**

**3 large mushrooms**

**250 ml/8 fl oz (1 cup) vegetable stock (broth)**

**150 g/5 oz smoked tofu (bean curd), mashed**

**1 bunch chives, finely chopped**

**1 tablespoon medium strength mustard**

**2 tablespoons crème fraîche**

**herb salt**

**1 bunch parsley**

**1 bunch chervil**

**50 g/2 oz watercress**

**3 sheets lovage**

**½ clove garlic, pressed**

**4 dashes soya sauce**

**4 tablespoons olive oil**

❶ Peel and quarter the tomatoes and remove the seeds. Blot the tomato pieces dry with kitchen paper. Wash the courgettes (zucchini) and cut into slices 2 cm/¾ in thick. Cut the slices across three times to make small triangles.

❷ Clean and dice the mushrooms. Pour 1 tablespoon of vegetable stock (broth) into a pan and braise the mushrooms briefly.

❸ Put the smoked tofu (bean curd), braised mushroom cubes, finely chopped chives, mustard and crème fraîche in a bowl and stir well. Season with herb salt. Cover and leave to marinate for 1–2 hours.

❹ To make the sauce: wash and dry the herbs. Pull the leaves off the stems. Purée the leaves of the herbs, garlic, soya sauce, herb salt and vegetable stock (broth) in a mixer to obtain a smooth mixture. Finally, add the olive oil little by little.

❺ Divide the herb sauce onto four plates. Shape the tofu (bean curd) mixture into 12 small balls and arrange three balls in a circle on the sauce. Arrange the tomato pieces on the soya balls so as to create a flower. Put the courgette (zucchini) triangles between the "petals" formed by the tomato pieces.

**Serves 4. About 188 kcal per serving**

**400 g/14 oz broccoli**

**300 g/10 oz cocktail tomatoes**

**2 slices cooked ham**

**100 g/3½ oz fresh shrimps**

**2 tablespoons white wine vinegar**

**1 tablespoon tomato ketchup**

**salt**

**pepper**

**6 tablespoons sunflower oil**

**100 ml/3½ fl oz (½ cup) cream**

# Tomato cocktail with shrimps and broccoli

Raw broccoli comes into its own in this salad made from tomatoes, shrimps and ham. Its nutty flavour gives the dish its finishing touch.

❶ Wash and prepare the broccoli and divide into bite-sized pieces. Halve the cocktail tomatoes and put in a large bowl with the broccoli. Cut the ham into fine strips and stir it into the vegetables together with the shrimps.

❷ For the salad dressing: whisk the ketchup and herbs vigorously with vinegar. Pour in the oil little by little while continuing to stir, then add the cream. Stir the mixture again until smooth and pour over the salad.

❸ Stir the dressing into the salad and leave to stand for about 20 minutes. Stir again just before serving and transfer into four small glass bowls.

**Serves 4. About 293 kcal per serving**

# Tomato omelette with basil and goat's cheese

A small snack for four people, but with ciabatta or French bread and a mixed salad, it makes a delicious light meal for two. A garnish of black olives completes this nourishing meal.

3 firm tomatoes

30 g/1 oz (2 tablespoons) butter

5 eggs

herb salt

freshly ground pepper

6 leaves fresh basil

80 g/3 oz goat's cheese, crumbled

❶ Peel and quarter the tomatoes; remove the seeds. Cut the tomato quarters into cubes. Melt 15 g/½ oz (1 tablespoon) butter in a saucepan, add the diced tomatoes and cook gently for 5 minutes. Leave to cool.

❷ Beat the eggs with herb salt and pepper in a bowl; stir in the tomatoes.

❸ Melt the remaining butter in a pan and make two omelettes from the egg and tomato mixture.

❹ Cut the omelettes in half and put on a warm plate. Garnish with basil and sprinkle the goat's cheese on top.

**Serves 4. About 208 kcal per serving**

# Tomato and rocket salad

Also known as rucola, rocket is known for giving a "kick" to any salad with its distinctive sharpness.

100 g/3½ oz rocket

800 g/1¾ lb medium tomatoes

120 g/4 oz (½ cup) green olives, stoned (pitted)

2 shallots

½ bunch basil

2 tablespoons balsamic vinegar

2 tablespoons vegetable stock (broth)

salt

black pepper from the mill

1 teaspoon dried Italian herbs

1 teaspoon honey

4 tablespoons basil-infused oil

2 packs mozzarella (200 g/7 oz each)

4 slices rye bread

❶ Tear the rocket into bite-sized pieces. Cut the tomatoes and drained olives into slices. Peel the shallots and dice very finely. Gently mix these ingredients together in a bowl with a few basil leaves.

❷ Pre-heat the oven to 220°C (425°F), Gas mark 7.

❸ For the salad dressing: mix together the vinegar, vegetable stock (broth), salt, pepper, Italian herbs and honey and stir vigorously. Lastly, add the oil. Pour the dressing over the tomato and rocket salad and mix well.

❹ Drain the mozzarella thoroughly, cut into slices and put these on the slices of bread. Sprinkle the remaining basil on the mozzarella and brown under the grill for about 5 minutes.

❺ Serve the tomato and rocket salad with the grilled mozzarella-topped slices of bread.

**Serves 4. About 533 kcal per serving**

# Tomatoes stuffed with asparagus, eggs and salad

From being a "party piece" in the 1970s, stuffed tomatoes have developed into a classic dish. A grapefruit knife with a curved, serrated blade makes it easier to hollow out the tomatoes.

❶ Hard-boil (hard-cook) an egg, allow to cool and shell. Drain the asparagus and peas.

❷ Cut the top off each tomato and carefully remove the flesh with a teaspoon. Sprinkle salt inside the hollowed-out tomatoes.

❸ Cut the spring onions (scallions) into slices about 1 cm/⅜ in thick. Dice the pork sausage, chop the eggs, cut the asparagus into small pieces, add the peas and stir. Add the dressing (see below). Fill the tomatoes with the salad mixture and put the top back on.

❹ For the dressing: mix the mayonnaise and yoghurt to make a smooth mixture. Add lemon juice and season with salt, sugar, cayenne pepper and paprika. Pour part of the dressing onto the salad stuffing and serve the rest separately.

**Serves 4. About 393 kcal per serving**

2 eggs

1 can asparagus pieces (150 g/5 oz)

1 can peas (150 g/5 oz)

8 beef tomatoes

salt

8 spring onions (scallions)

250 g/9 oz pork sausage

5 tablespoons yoghurt

3 tablespoons mayonnaise

1 dash lemon juice

sugar

cayenne pepper

paprika

# Tomato salad with bananas

2 ripe bananas

1 tablespoon lemon juice

500 g/18 oz firm tomatoes

2 tablespoons balsamic vinegar

6 tablespoons sunflower oil

½ teaspoon medium strength
   mustard

salt

pepper

curry powder

sugar

1 bunch smooth parsley

This red and yellow salad will add an exotic touch to the table. Served in a hollowed-out pineapple, it will conjure up images of the Caribbean.

❶ Peel and slice the bananas and sprinkle with lemon juice. Peel the tomatoes, cut in half and slice. Put the tomato and banana slices in a bowl and mix together carefully.

❷ For the salad dressing: mix the vinegar, oil and mustard together and stir vigorously. Season to taste with salt, pepper, curry powder and sugar. Pour the dressing over the salad and stir gently.

❸ Arrange the salad on four plates and sprinkle with chopped parsley.

**Serves 4. About 236 kcal per serving**

# Courgette (zucchini) and tomato salad

4 eggs

1 bunch smooth parsley

100 g/3½ oz (1 cup) Parmesan

300 g/10 oz courgettes (zucchini)

500 g/18 oz plum tomatoes

3 teaspoons balsamic vinegar

5 teaspoons sunflower oil

1 pinch sugar

salt

red pepper from the mill

Courgette (zucchini) and tomato salad is a nourishing, tasty combination of vegetables and eggs which can also be served as a main meal.

❶ Hard-boil (hard cook) the eggs, allow to cool and cut into slices. Coarsely chop the parsley. Grate the Parmesan.

❷ Peel and slice the courgettes (zucchini). Slice the tomatoes. Put the vegetables in a large bowl.

❸ To make the dressing: mix the oil and vinegar, add the sugar and season to taste, stirring well. Pour over the vegetables. Add the sliced eggs and stir very gently.

❹ Sprinkle the tomato and courgette (zucchini) salad with parsley and shavings of Parmesan.

**Serves 4. About 286 kcal per serving**

# Soups and stews

Soups tend to be simple, while a stew frequently combines several vegetable and meat ingredients. A stew makes a delicious and nourishing meal for your guests, for instance Lamb and tomato stew (page 49), while a soup such as Creamed tomato soup with wine (page 42) is perfect as a light starter (appetizer). An interesting feature of stew is that it tastes even better when reheated the day after it is made, having marinated longer. Soups too can be kept in the refrigerator, and frozen if they have not been thickened with flour.

# Tomato and bacon soup

This rich, nourishing soup tastes best when prepared with very ripe beef tomatoes. In winter, these can be replaced by canned tomatoes. In that case it will not be necessary to strain the soup; it can simply be puréed with a hand-mixer.

4 small onions

1 kg/2¼ lb tomatoes

1–2 cloves garlic

80 g/3 oz streaky bacon

40 g/1½ oz (6 tablespoons) flour

750 ml/1¼ pints (3½ cups) beef stock (broth)

salt

freshly ground pepper

paprika pepper

chopped thyme

100 ml/3½ fl oz (½ cup) cream

a few leaves of basil as garnish

❶ Peel the onions and chop finely. Peel the tomatoes, cut into quarters and remove the seeds. Peel and press the cloves of garlic.

❷ Cut the bacon into small dice and melt in a pan. Add the chopped onion and sweat until transparent. Sprinkle the flour on top and brown lightly. Add the tomato pieces to the pan and braise briefly. Pour the beef stock (broth) over all.

❸ Season the soup with salt, pepper, paprika, thyme and garlic. Cover and simmer on a low heat for 15 minutes.

❹ Beat the cream until semi-stiff. Strain the soup through a sieve and return to the pan. Reheat and season again. Pour into bowls and garnish with a spoonful of cream and basil leaves.

**Serves 4. About 350 kcal per serving**

# Tomato consommé

Clear tomato soup is quite unusual, but it must be carefully prepared. The soup is clarified by pouring it through a cloth; after that it must not be stirred, nor must the vegetables pushed through the cloth, or the soup will become cloudy.

1 onion

1 small container pickled, green peppercorns

1 leek

½ bunch smooth parsley

2 egg whites

2 jugs beef stock (broth), 500 ml/17 fl oz (2¼ cups) each

1 bay leaf

1 can chopped tomatoes with juice (400 g/14 oz)

salt

sugar

❶ Grate the onion finely. Remove the green peppercorns from the brine and crush with a fork. Wash the leek and cut into slices. Coarsely chop the parsley. Mix the egg whites with 500 ml/17 fl oz (2 cups) of cold beef stock (broth).

❷ Pour the beef stock (broth) – both that with the egg whites and that without – into a large saucepan. Add the onion, crushed peppercorns, leek, bay leaves, chopped tomatoes and juice. Bring to the boil, stirring frequently. Season to taste with salt and sugar. Reduce the heat and simmer for about 50 minutes without the lid.

❸ Line a colander with a clean cotton tea towel and strain the soup. Do not push the vegetables through.

❹ Reheat the tomato consommé. Pour into soup bowls and sprinkle with parsley.

**Serves 4. About 115 kcal per serving**

# Cold tomato soup

800 g/1¾ lb ripe beef tomatoes

1 red pepper

½ cucumber

1 small red onion

1 small red chilli pepper

1 clove garlic, pressed

200 ml/7 fl oz (⅞ cup) vegetable stock (broth)

2 tablespoons wine vinegar

2 tablespoons olive oil

250 ml/8 fl oz (1 cup) tomato juice (see page 131)

herb salt

freshly ground white pepper

soya sauce

1 piece cucumber, peeled

½ yellow pepper, deseeded

rocket, finely chopped

A spicy yet refreshing light starter (appetizer) for a hot summer's day. Delicious with freshly baked white bread.

❶ Peel the tomatoes, cut the red pepper into four and remove the seeds. Peel the cucumbers, cut in half lengthways and remove the seeds with a teaspoon. Peel the onion.

❷ Chop the tomatoes, red pepper, cucumber, onion and chilli pepper coarsely and mix together. Put this mixture through the mincer (grinder) or chop with the hand-mixer. Add the garlic, vegetable stock (broth), vinegar, oil and tomato juice and stir.

❸ Season the soup with herb salt, white pepper and spiced soya sauce. Cover and put in a cool place for at least 2 hours.

❹ Just before serving, cut the yellow pepper and cucumber into strips and garnish the soup with them. Sprinkle with finely chopped rocket.

**Serves 4. About 120 kcal per servings**

# Tomato soup with sherry

2 onions

500 g/18 oz ripe tomatoes

4 carrots

40 g/1½ oz (3 tablespoons) clarified butter

salt

½ teaspoon dried herbs of Provence

1 bay leaf

250 ml/8 fl oz (1 cup) tomato juice

500 ml/17 fl oz (2¼ cups) beef stock (broth)

pepper

200 ml/7 fl oz (⅞ cup) sherry

4 teaspoons crème fraîche

The celebrated Spanish wine of sherry is often used to flavour soups and sauces because of its distinctive bouquet.

❶ Peel and chop the onions. Peel the tomatoes and cut into quarters. Peel the carrots and cut into slices. Heat the clarified butter in a large saucepan. Add the chopped onions and season with salt and herbs of Provence. Cook for a few minutes.

❷ Add the tomatoes, carrots and bay leaves to the saucepan and cook for a few more minutes. Add the tomato juice and beef stock (broth) to the vegetable mixture and bring to the boil. Reduce the heat and season the soup with salt and pepper. Cover and simmer for another 45 minutes.

❸ Remove the vegetables from the saucepan with a perforated spoon and purée in the blender. Return this purée to the soup, stir and reheat. Add the sherry and season again if necessary.

❹ Pour the soup into bowls and garnish with a teaspoon of crème fraîche.

**Serves 4. About 215 kcal per serving**

# Tomato soup
# with cheese balls

Tomato and cheese are a perfect combination in soups as well as in starters (appetizers) or salads. The flavour of this delicious soup, made with ripe outdoor tomatoes is enhanced by the addition of cheese balls.

750 g/1¾ lb beef tomatoes

½ teaspoon chopped thyme

½ teaspoon chopped rosemary

salt

freshly ground pepper

sugar

a few leaves of celery

1 onion

1 tablespoon olive oil

1 tablespoon flour

5 tablespoons cream

3 tablespoons leaves of basil, cut into strips

For the cheese balls:

200 g/7 oz double (heavy) cream curd cheese

100 g/3½ oz (1 cup) freshly grated Parmesan

1 egg

2 tablespoons flour

1 pinch salt

1 pinch cayenne pepper

❶ Peel and quarter the tomatoes; remove the seeds. Dice the tomato quarters very small. Put 750 ml/1¼ pints (3¼ cups) water in a saucepan and add the tomatoes, herbs, ½ teaspoon salt, ½ teaspoon pepper, 1 pinch of sugar and celery leaves. Bring to the boil. Cover and simmer for 20 minutes.

❷ To make the cheese balls: mix curd cheese, Parmesan, egg and flour. Season with salt and cayenne pepper. Cover the mixture and put in the refrigerator.

❸ Peel the onions and chop finely. Pour the tomato soup through a fine sieve and return the liquid to the pan. Rub the tomatoes through the sieve. Heat the olive oil in a pan and fry the onion until golden-brown. Sprinkle flour into the pan and cook until it turns a light brown colour. Add the puréed tomatoes, stir well and simmer on a low heat for 5 minutes. Pour this tomato mixture into the soup, stir well and bring back to the boil.

❹ Bring some salted water to the boil. Using a teaspoon, make cheese balls from the cheese mixture and cook in the boiling water for 2 minutes.

❺ Add the cream to the soup and season to taste with salt, pepper and sugar. Add the basil and stir into the soup. Serve in a soup tureen or directly in soup bowls. Garnish with the cheese balls.

**Serves 4. About 417 kcal per serving**

# Gazpacho

The Spanish speciality gazpacho is a refreshing vegetable soup which is served ice-cold. It can also be diluted with ice-cold water. The soup is eaten with croutons, diced cucumber, red peppers, tomatoes and onions served in bowls on the table.

800 g/1¾ lb ripe tomatoes

2 onions

2–3 cloves garlic

1 cucumber

1 green pepper

1 red pepper

3 tablespoons olive oil

1 tablespoon wine vinegar

salt

freshly ground pepper

2–3 slices white bread, crusts removed

25 g/1 oz (2 tablespoons) butter

❶ Peel and quarter the tomatoes and remove the seeds. Peel the onions and garlic. Peel the cucumber and cut in half lengthways; remove the seeds and dice. Cut the red pepper in half, remove the seeds and cut into eight pieces.

❷ Cut one-third of the tomatoes, onions, garlic, cucumber and red pepper into small cubes. Purée the rest in the blender with oil and vinegar and season with salt and pepper. Pour the gazpacho in a bowl, cover and put in the refrigerator.

❸ Just before serving, cut slices of white bread into small cubes. Heat some butter in a pan and fry the bread cubes until golden brown. Put in a small bowl like the other diced vegetables and serve with the soup.

**Serves 4. About 250 kcal per serving**

# Creamed tomato soup with wine

The wine adds a special touch to this dish, enhancing the flavour of this traditional tomato soup with delicious results.

200 g/7 oz cooked ham

2 tablespoons oil

1 can tomatoes (400 g/14 oz)

500 ml/17 fl oz (2¼ cups) beef stock (broth)

200 ml/7 fl oz (⅞ cup) white wine

200 g/7 oz curd cheese

100 g/3½ oz crème fraîche

2 tablespoons tomato purée

salt

pepper

❶ Cut the ham into small cubes. Heat the oil in a large pan and fry the diced ham briefly.

❷ Pour the tomatoes through a sieve and reserve the liquid. Dice the tomatoes. Put the diced tomatoes and juice into a saucepan and stir. Add the beef stock (broth) and wine. Bring the soup to the boil and simmer for about 15 minutes.

❸ Put the curd cheese, crème fraîche and tomato purée in a bowl and stir until the mixture is smooth. Add 2 cups of stock (broth) to this mixture and stir well. Stir the crème fraîche into the soup and bring back to the boil. Season the tomato soup to taste with salt and pepper.

**Serves 4. About 485 kcal per serving**

# Traditional tomato soup

This delicious tomato soup is ideal as a starter (appetizer), a snack or a light evening meal.

3 shallots

2 tablespoons vegetable oil

500 g/18 oz ripe tomatoes

750 ml/1¼ pints (3½ cups) vegetable stock (broth)

25 g/1 oz (2 tablespoons) butter

1 tablespoon flour

100 g/3½ oz crème fraîche

salt

pepper

sugar

❶ Coarsely chop the shallots. Heat the oil in large saucepan and sweat the chopped shallots. Put one tablespoon aside for the garnish.

❷ Cut the tomatoes into four, remove the seeds and add to the shallots in the saucepan. Cook briefly while stirring continuously. Add the vegetable stock (broth) and simmer for about 20 minutes. Strain the soup through a sieve and put to one side.

❸ Melt the butter in a large saucepan, carefully add the flour and stir vigorously with a whisk. Next add the soup liquid little by little making sure there are no lumps.

❹ Stir the crème fraîche into the tomato soup. Season to taste.

**Serves 4. About 332 kcal per serving**

# Bread soup with tomatoes

This bread soup with tomatoes is spicy and nourishing. The peppers and garlic give it its piquant flavour, while the white bread and tomatoes provide the bulk which makes it so nourishing.

2 peppers

2 cloves garlic

1 bunch parsley

150 g/5 oz white bread

3 shallots

2 tablespoons olive oil

1 large can tomatoes (800 g/1¾ lb)

500 ml/17 fl oz (2¼ cups) vegetable stock (broth)

salt

pepper

some olive oil with spices

❶ Remove the seeds from the peppers and cut into narrow strips. Peel the garlic and cut into wafer-thin slices. Chop the parsley. Remove the crusts and cut the bread into strips about 1.5 cm/½ in thick.

❷ Peel and chop the shallots. Heat some oil in a large saucepan and fry the chopped shallots lightly.

❸ Add the tomatoes and juice, peppers, parsley and garlic to the saucepan. Mash the tomatoes with a fork until smooth. Stir well and add the vegetable stock (broth). Season with salt and pepper. Bring the soup to the boil, stir, reduce the heat and simmer for about 15 minutes.

❹ Add the bread strips to the soup and continue simmering for another 10 minutes. Pour the soup into the bowls and add a dash of olive oil to each one.

**Serves 4. About 197 kcal per serving**

# Tomato and orange soup

The chicken broth for this soup is very easy to make – all it needs is some time. Boil 1 boiling fowl in 2½ litres/4¼ pints (11 cups) of water, skimming regularly to remove the foam. Add a bunch of soup vegetables (carrots, celery, leeks and parsley ), 1 small peeled onion stuck with three cloves, 1 small bunch of tarragon, salt and pepper. Simmer the stock (broth) for 1½ hours, then pour through a sieve. Leave to cool and remove any fat which has formed on top.

**1** Peel the onion and garlic, slice the onion and press the garlic. Peel the potatoes and cut into dice. Peel the tomatoes, cut into four pieces and remove the seeds. Chop up the tomato pieces.

**2** Heat some oil in a saucepan. Add the onion rings and diced potatoes and fry gently while stirring continuously for 2–3 minutes until the onion is transparent.

**3** Add the tomatoes, tarragon and garlic. Add the chicken stock (broth) and season with salt and pepper. Bring to the boil and simmer on a low heat for about 20–25 minutes.

**4** Purée the soup in a liquidizer or hand-mixer, add the orange juice and grated zest and reheat. The soup can be served hot or cold.

**Serves 4. About 130 kcal per serving**

1 onion

1 clove garlic

1 potato

1,5 kg/3¼ lb tomatoes

2 tablespoons oil

4 teaspoons chopped tarragon

500 ml/17 fl oz (2¼ cups) chicken stock (broth)

salt

freshly ground pepper

250 ml/8 fl oz (1 cup) orange juice

1 teaspoon grated orange peel

# Spicy tomato soup
# with avocado and shrimps

Originating in Mexico, this delicious soup is also much appreciated elsewhere. It is a spicy tomato soup, pleasantly warming in colder climates and an excellent addition to any party menu.

1 red onion

2 large cans tomatoes
   (800 g/1¾ lb each)

5 tablespoons olive oil

2 cloves garlic

½ teaspoon oregano

½ teaspoon chilli powder

salt

1 teaspoon powdered vegetable
   stock (broth)

1 tablespoon sugar

4 slices white bread

1 avocado

juice of 1 lemon

1 yellow pepper

2 tablespoons chopped parsley

a few dashes of Tabasco

100 g/3½ oz shrimps

1 tablespoon chopped basil

❶ Chop the onions coarsely. Strain the tomatoes through a sieve and reserve the juice.

❷ Heat 2 tablespoons oil in a large saucepan. Add the diced onion, 1 pressed clove of garlic, and fry lightly. Add the strained tomatoes and juice and stir. Add the vegetable stock (broth) and season with oregano, chilli powder, salt and sugar; simmer for about 10 minutes. Taste and season again if necessary.

❸ Remove the crusts of the slices of white bread and cut into small cubes. Heat the remaining oil in a pan and fry the diced bread; add 1 pressed garlic clove and put to one side.

❹ Halve the avocado lengthways, remove the stone (seed) and take out the flesh with a spoon. Dice the avocado flesh, put in a bowl and sprinkle immediately with half the lemon juice.

❺ Wash the yellow pepper, cut into dice and add to the diced avocado. Add the chopped parsley and mix well. Season generously with salt and tabasco.

❻ Put the shrimps in a bowl and stir in the chopped basil and the remaining lemon juice. Serve the croutons and avocado mixture separately in bowls to accompany the soup.

**Serves 4. About 295 kcal per serving**

# Tomato and garlic soup

This soup owes its name to the ten cloves of garlic used in preparing it. Because eight of the cloves are removed shortly before the soup is ready, the garlic is not overwhelming.

10 cloves garlic

1 red onion

2 tablespoons oil

2 cans chopped tomatoes (400 g/14 oz each)

500 ml/17 fl oz (2¼ cups) beef stock (broth)

200 ml tomato juice

1 bay leaf

1 tablespoon sweet soya sauce

1 teaspoon balsamic vinegar

1 pinch sugar

salt

pepper

100 g/3½ oz crème fraîche

1 handful basil leaves

❶ Peel the garlic and the onions; cut the onion in rings.

❷ Heat the oil in a large saucepan and lightly fry the onion rings and cloves of garlic.

❸ Add the chopped tomatoes with the juice to the onion and garlic. Stir and add the beef stock (broth), tomato juice and bay leaves. Season with soya sauce, vinegar, sugar, salt and pepper. Bring to the boil and stir. Reduce the heat and and simmer for about 30 minutes.

❹ Using a perforated spoon, remove the bay leaves and garlic cloves from the soup. Using a fork, mash two of the cloves and return to the soup. Stir in the crème fraîche. Taste and season if necessary and simmer for another 5 minutes. Garnish with the basil leaves.

**Serves 4. About 239 kcal per serving**

# Tomato and lamb stew

A delicious, nourishing stew made with lamb, tomatoes, herbs, spices and red wine. This filling dish will satisfy the hungriest guests.

❶ Peel the tomatoes, cut into quarters and remove the seeds. Peel the onions and cloves of garlic; cut the onions into rings and chop the cloves finely. Using a sharp knife, remove the fat and skin from the lamb and cut into bite-sized pieces. Chop the parsley.

❷ Warm the oil in a large saucepan. Briefly fry the onion rings and garlic. Add the meat and sear until well browned, stirring continuously. Add the tomato ketchup, salt, pepper, thyme and rosemary; stir again. Add the red wine and stock (broth). Bring to the boil and simmer gently for about 30 minutes.

❸ Add the tomatoes, olives and parsley to the stew and stir; simmer for another 10 minutes. Remove the rosemary. Season to taste. Garnish with parsley just before serving.

**Serves 4. About 451 kcal per serving**

400 g/14 oz tomatoes
100 g/3½ oz red onions
3 cloves garlic
500 g/18 oz shoulder of lamb
½ bunch smooth parsley
4 tablespoons olive oil
2 tablespoons tomato ketchup
salt
pepper
½ teaspoon chopped thyme
1 sprig rosemary
250 ml/8 fl oz (1 cup) red wine
750 ml/1¼ pints (3½ cups) vegetable stock (broth)
80 g/3 oz green olives, stoned (pitted)

# Green (snap) bean and tomato stew

This green (snap) bean and tomato stew is very nourishing and an ideal winter dish. The fragrance of the savory which develops during the cooking makes this dish particularly heart-warming on a cold winter's day.

❶ Peel and slice the onions and garlic. Peel the tomatoes and cut into bite-sized pieces.

❷ Heat the oil in a large saucepan and lightly fry the onions and garlic . Stir in the tomato ketchup. Add the chopped tomatoes and fry briefly.

❸ Drain the green (snap) beans and add to the stew. Add the vegetable stock (broth) and season with vinegar, salt and pepper. Add the savory and bring the mixture to the boil. Reduce the heat and simmer for about 30 minutes, stirring now and again.

❹ When the stew is cooked, remove the savory and season to taste.

**Serves 4. About 161 kcal per serving**

2 onions

4 cloves garlic

800 g/1¾ lb beef tomatoes

2 tablespoons olive oil

2 tablespoons tomato ketchup

1 can green (snap) beans (400 g/14 oz)

1 litre/1¾ pints (4½ cups) vegetable stock (broth)

2 teaspoons balsamic vinegar

salt

white pepper

1 sprig savory

# Cucumber and tomato stew with meatballs

This stew made with cucumbers, tomatoes, mushrooms and crème fraîche is a dish which will please everyone.

❶ Drain the mushrooms thoroughly. Peel the cucumbers, cut into half, remove the seeds and slice; cut the tomatoes into quarters.

❷ Season the minced (ground) pork with salt and pepper and make it into small meat balls. Heat the cooking fat in a pan and fry the meat balls all over until well browned. Remove from the pan and put aside.

❸ Heat the oil in a large saucepan. Briefly fry the mixed mushrooms and cucumber. Add the chopped tomatoes, stir and cover with the vegetable stock (broth). Bring to the boil and simmer on a low heat for about 20 minutes.

❹ Add the meat balls and dill to the liquid and stir in the crème fraîche. Season to taste with salt and pepper.

**Serves 4. About 358 kcal per serving**

1 can mixed mushrooms (300 g/10 oz)

3 small cucumbers

500 g/18 oz beef tomatoes

250 g/9 oz minced (ground) pork

pepper

salt

3 teaspoons cooking fat

2 tablespoons oil

750 ml/1¼ pints (3½ cups) vegetable stock (broth)

1 tablespoon chopped dill

3 tablespoons crème fraîche

# Pickles
# and preserves

Preserved in spiced vinegar or a mixture of oil and vinegar, tomatoes make delicious pickles. Before being eaten, the pickle should be left for a day or two in its marinade in the refrigerator so that the special taste given to the tomatoes by the other ingredients can develop well. Pickles may be hot, such as Chilli tomatoes (page 58), or intensely flavoured with herbs, such as cocktail tomatoes in tarragon vinegar (page 58).

People with a liking for unusual preserves will enjoy the excellent Tomato jam (preserve) recipe (page 60).

1 kg/2¼ lb beef tomatoes

12 spring onions (scallions)

2 cloves garlic

3 tablespoons basil-infused oil

1 tablespoon raspberry vinegar

½ teaspoon dried Italian herbs

1 teaspoon brown sugar

salt

# Bottled tomatoes

No special cooking equipment is needed to bottle tomatoes – just an ordinary oven will do. You can decide for yourself what to bottle with the tomatoes: shallots, red onions, white onions, spring onions (scallions), garlic, sliced leeks, sliced carrots, strips of celery, and so on.

❶ Peel the tomatoes, cut into quarters and remove the seeds. Peel the onions and cut in half. Peel the garlic and chop finely.

❷ Pre-heat the oven to 180°C/350°F, Gas mark 4. Fill a deep roasting tin with 3 cm/1¼ in water.

❸ Heat the oil in a large saucepan and briefly fry the onions and garlic. Add the tomato pieces, vinegar, herbs, sugar, salt and pepper; heat up again, stirring all the time. Continue cooking the vegetables for another 15 minutes, stirring now and again. Season to taste.

❹ Fill four preserving jars, each of about 250 ml/8 oz (2 cups), with the tomato mixture and put in the roasting tin. Put it on the bottom shelf of the oven. As soon as the tomato mixture starts to bubble, reduce the oven temperature to 150°C/300°F, Gas mark 2. Take the jars out of the oven after 30 minutes.

**Makes 4 jars. About 152 kcal per jar**

# Vodka cherry tomatoes

This will add a Russian note to your dinner party. It is a perfect way of refreshing the palate between courses.

500 g/18 oz cherry tomatoes

2 small containers pickled, green peppercorns

1 cup vodka

4 tablespoons herb salt

1 tablespoon white pepper from the mill

1 lemon

❶ Prick the cherry tomatoes all over with toothpick. Remove the peppercorns from the brine and crush with the back of the knife. Reserve the brine.

❷ Pour the vodka into a dish, add the brine and pepper. Put the cherry tomatoes in it next to each other. Cover with cling film and leave in the refrigerator for 2 hours.

❸ Put the herb salt and white pepper in a bowl, mix well and serve as a dip for the cherry tomatoes. Cut the lemon into eight pieces and garnish the herb salt with them. Drain the cherry tomatoes before serving.

**Makes 4 jars. About 83 kcal per jar**

# Green tomatoes in ginger vinegar

Ginger and cinnamon are the ideal condiments for preserves and jam, and they give green tomatoes an almost Oriental flavour. Served with the Indian flat unleavened bread, nan, green tomatoes in ginger vinegar make an excellent entrée or starter (appetizer) for an Indian meal.

1 piece fresh ginger (about 6 cm/2½ in)

1 kg/2¼ lb soft green tomatoes (already showing some traces of orange)

2 tablespoons salt

1 litre/1¾ pints (4½ cups) red wine vinegar

500 g/18 oz (2½ cups) brown sugar

1 tablespoon black peppercorns

1 cinnamon stick

❶ Peel the ginger and slice finely. Cut the tomatoes into quarters and remove the seeds. Bring 2 litres/3½ pints (9 cups) of salted water to the boil and add the tomatoes. Using a perforated spoon, remove the tomatoes from the boiling water after about 2 minutes. Leave to cool for a moment and remove the skins. Put the peeled tomatoes in four preserving jars each of about 500 ml/17 fl oz (2¼ cups).

❷ Pour the red wine vinegar into a pan, add the sugar, peppercorns, cinnamon sticks and ginger and bring to boil, stirring continuously. Simmer for about 5 minutes, stirring now and again.

❸ Remove the cinnamon sticks from the liquid. Pour the hot liquid over the tomatoes. Cover the jars, leave to cool and store in the refrigerator. Use within eight weeks.

**Makes 4 jars. About 59 kcal per jar**

# Cocktail tomatoes in tarragon vinegar

Do not throw away the vinegar when you have finished the tomatoes; it is delicious in salad dressings!

1 kg/2¼ lb cherry tomatoes

4 cloves garlic

4 litres/7 pints (18 cups) white wine vinegar

3 sprigs tarragon

1 teaspoon powdered allspice

❶ Prick the cherry tomatoes all over with a toothpick. Peel the cloves of garlic.

❷ Pour the vinegar into a large saucepan, add the tarragon, cloves of garlic and allspice berries. Bring to the boil and cook for about 10 minutes. Leave to cool and pour through a sieve, so as to separate the vinegar from the other ingredients.

❸ Take 4 preserving jars each of about 1 litre/1¾ pints (4½ cups) and put the tomatoes in them. Fill each glass with the vinegar to within 2 cm/¾ in of the top. Cover the jars and store in the refrigerator.

❹ Leave the cocktail tomatoes to marinate for a few days in the seasoned vinegar. Stored in a cold place, the bottled tomatoes can be kept for about 8 weeks.

**Makes 4 jars. About 47 kcal per jar**

# Bottled chilli tomatoes

As well as being a mouth-watering snack, chilli tomatoes are delicious served with fried meat.

1 kg/2¼ lb ripe, firm tomatoes

4 shallots

4 cloves garlic

4 chillis, chopped

1 litre/1¾ pints (4½ cups) balsamic vinegar

2 bay leaves

❶ Cut the tomatoes into quarters and remove the seeds. Peel the shallots and cut into four. Peel the garlic and cut into half.

❷ Divide the tomatoes, shallots and garlic between four preserving jars each of about 500 ml/17 fl oz (2¼ cups). Add a chilli pepper to each one.

❸ Heat the balsamic vinegar in a saucepan with the bay leaves. Simmer for a few minutes. Remove the bay leaves and pour the vinegar into the jars, completely covering the tomatoes, shallots and garlic.

❹ Leave the chilli tomatoes to marinate for three days before eating. Store the jars in the refrigerator and use within 8 weeks.

**Makes 4 jars. About 96 kcal per jar**

# Sun-dried tomatoes with pears in garlic oil

This unusual combination of tomatoes and pears is delicious with a cheese raclette, for instance. It makes a pleasant change from the traditional mixed pickles usually served with a raclette.

500 g/18 oz dried tomatoes in oil

1 can pears (400 g/14 oz)

4 cloves garlic

½ bunch thyme

300 ml/10 fl oz (1¼ cups) apple vinegar

750 ml/1¼ pints (3½ cups) vegetable oil

sugar

salt

pepper

❶ Remove the sun-dried tomatoes from the oil, rinse briefly and wipe dry with kitchen paper. Drain the pears and cut into slices 2 cm/¾ in thick. Peel the garlic and cut into thin, diagonal slivers.

❷ Divide the tomatoes, pears, garlic and thyme into four preserving jars each of about 500 ml/17 fl oz (2¼ cups).

❸ Mix the oil, vinegar, sugar, salt and pepper to make a marinade. Season to taste and pour into the preserving jars to cover all the ingredients. Cover the jars and leave to marinate in the refrigerator for one day before eating. Keep the bottled sun-dried tomatoes in the refrigerator and eat within four days.

**Makes 4 jars. About 125 kcal per jar**

# Tomato jam (preserve)

Tomato jam (preserve) is a delicious snack that can be enjoyed at any time of the day, on white bread or on coarse brown bread.

1 kg/2¼ lb ripe tomatoes

2 cm/1 in fresh root ginger

grated peel of 1 orange

juice of 1 lemon

1 kg/2¼ lb (5 cups) pectin sugar

❶ Coarsely chop the tomatoes and put in a saucepan. Add 200 ml/7 fl oz (⅞ cup) water and bring to the boil. Simmer for 10 minutes. Pass through a sieve, return to the saucepan and leave to cool.

❷ Peel the ginger, slice thinly and chop very finely. Add the ginger together with the orange zest, lemon juice and preserving sugar (containing pectin) to the mashed tomatoes. Boil the jam (preserve) vigorously over a high heat for 5 minutes until it sets.

❸ Pour the hot tomato jam (preserve) immediately into jars with a screw-top lid. Allow to cool down upside down.

**Makes about 500 g/18 oz jam (preserve), containing about 4,245 kcal.**

# Cherry tomatoes preserved with olives and sheep's milk cheese

500 g/18 oz cherry tomatoes

500 g/18 oz sheep's milk cheese

1 bunch smooth parsley

1 clove garlic

60 g/2 oz black olives, stoned (pitted)

60 g/2 oz green olives, stoned (pitted)

150 ml/5 fl oz (⅝ cup) wine vinegar

500 ml/17 fl oz (2¼ cups) olive oil

salt

coloured pepper from the mill

sugar

Bottled tomatoes are an ideal nibble to serve with an aperitif of still or sparkling wine. They can be served in small bowls and eaten with a fork.

❶ Prick the tomatoes all over with a toothpick. Cut up the sheep's milk cheese into cubes of 2 cm/¾ in.

❷ Coarsely chop the parsley, peel the garlic and slice into thin shavings. Fill a large jar of 1.5 litres/2¾ pints (7 cups) with alternate layers of sheep's milk cheese, tomatoes, olives, garlic and herbs.

❸ To make the marinade: mix the oil and vinegar and season with salt, pepper and sugar. Pour the marinade into the preserving jar to cover all the ingredients.

❹ Cover the jar with cling film and leave in the fridge to marinate for one day. Store in a cool place. Use within four days.

**Serves 4. About 402 kcal per serving**

# A variety of side dishes

Tomato dishes make a perfect accompaniment for roast meat, fried or grilled fish, and simple potato dishes. The versatile tomato can be prepared as a sauce – Mashed potato gratin with tomato sauce (page 77), or stuffed – Stuffed tomatoes with rice and sultanas (golden raisins) (page 79), or baked as vegetable in the oven – Tomatoes à la Provençale (page 72), or served as a fried vegetable – Fried green tomatoes with béchamel sauce (page 74). Bread garnished with a tomato-based topping is also delicious and can be eaten as a quick snack or a light evening meal.

# Gnocchi with tomatoes and sage

Gnocchi are Italian potato dumplings made with boiled potatoes, egg yolks and flour. They only take a few minutes to cook in boiling water and are delicious served with a tomato sauce.

1 kg/2¼ lb potatoes, cooked floury

1 kg/2¼ lb ripe medium tomatoes

2 shallots

2 tablespoons sunflower oil

salt

pepper

3 egg yolks

200 g/7 oz (2 cups) flour

15 g/½ oz (1 tablespoon) butter

12 leaves of sage

50 g/2 oz (½ cup) grated Pecorino

❶ Boil the potatoes. unpeeled, for 20–25 minutes until soft.

❷ Cut the tomatoes into quarters, remove the seeds and dice. Peel the shallots and chop finely.

❸ Heat the oil in a pan. Add the chopped shallots and sweat until transparent. Now add the diced tomatoes, stir and season with salt and pepper. Simmer the tomato mixture on a medium heat for about 10 minutes until the tomatoes are cooked. Taste and adjust the seasoning if necessary.

❹ Bring about 2 litres/3½ pints (9 cups) salted water to the boil in a large saucepan.

❺ Peel the potatoes while they are still hot and put them on a plate. Mash them thoroughly with a fork. Add the egg yolks, salt and flour and knead into the mashed potatoes until the mixture is smooth. Using a teaspoon, take small amounts of this potato and flour dough and shape into small balls, rolling each one between the palms of your hand. Flatten the gnocchi slightly with a fork and cook them a few at a time in boiling water for about 4 minutes. Remove with a perforated spoon.

❻ Melt the butter in a saucepan and fry the sage briefly. Toss the gnocchi in the butter and sage and put on individual plates. Serve with tomato sauce and Pecorino cheese.

**Serves 4. About 539 kcal per serving**

# Tomatoes with basil and crème fraîche

A kitchen without basil seems unthinkable today. Fresh basil leaves have a particularly powerful aroma which combines beautifully with tomatoes. If dried basil is used, the flavour will be pleasant but different: dried basil tastes a little like aniseed.

250 g/9 oz red onions

2 cloves garlic

8 beef tomatoes

butter for the mould

25 g/1 oz (2 tablespoons) clarified butter

125 ml/4 fl oz (½ cup) vegetable stock (broth)

125 ml/4 fl oz (½ cup) Prosecco or other sparkling wine

250 ml/8 fl oz (1 cup) crème fraîche

salt

lemon pepper

1 handful leaves of basil

50 g/2 oz (⅔ cup) pine nuts

50 g/2 oz (½ cup) grated Parmesan

❶ Peel the onions and the garlic. Chop finely. Peel the tomatoes.

❷ Pre-heat the oven to 220°C (425°F), Gas mark 7. Butter a baking dish generously.

❸ Heat the clarified butter in a pan and fry the chopped onion and garlic. Add the vegetable stock (broth) and Prosecco and stir. Simmer for about 10 minutes.

❹ Stir in the crème fraîche and continue cooking the sauce while stirring. Season with salt and pepper. Then stir in the basil leaves and pine nuts.

❺ Put the tomatoes stalk end downwards in the baking dish. Make a cross-shaped incision in the top of each tomato. Pour the crème fraîche and basil over the tomatoes and sprinkle with Parmesan.

❻ Put the baking dish in the middle of the oven and bake for 15–20 minutes.

**Serves 4. About 270 kcal per serving**

# Spaghetti with cherry tomatoes

A simple but delicious dish which only takes half an hour to prepare. Instead of spaghetti spiral-shaped pasta, tagliatelli, farfalle, penne or even wholemeal (whole wheat) pasta can be used. The latter is particularly rich in fibre and B-vitamins.

**1** Pre-heat the oven to 220°C/425°F, Gas mark 7. Peel the garlic and chop finely. Stir the olive oil, garlic, basil and parsley together in a small bowl.

**2** Put the tomatoes in a large baking tin. Pour seasoned oil over the tomatoes. Sprinkle with herb salt and pepper. Cook the tomatoes in the pre-heated oven for 10 minutes.

**3** Boil the spaghetti in plenty of salted water following the instructions until cooked al dente. Add the peas 3 minutes before the end of the cooking time.

**4** Drain the spaghetti and peas, reserving 250 ml/8 fl oz (1 cup) of the cooking water in a bowl.

**5** Stir the cooking water into the curd cheese and beat with a whisk to make a creamy sauce. Season to taste.

**6** Add the mixture of spaghetti and peas to the cherry tomatoes in the baking tin. Pour the cheese sauce over it and stir well. Season again with salt and pepper and serve hot.

**Serves 4. About 663 kcal per serving**

**1 clove garlic**
**3 tablespoons olive oil**
**1 tablespoon chopped basil**
**1 tablespoon chopped parsley**
**500 g/18 oz cherry tomatoes**
**spiced oil**
**herb salt**
**freshly ground pepper**
**500 g/18 oz spaghetti**
**salt**
**150 g/5 oz peas**
**150 g/5 oz curd cheese with feta**

# Ravioli with tomatoes

Ravioli, the small squares of pasta stuffed with meat, ham, cheese or spinach, can be bought ready-made. Tortellini are similar, shaped like small pasta rounds, containing similar fillings to those used in ravioli.

❶ Drain the tomatoes in a colander and catch the juice in a bowl. Coarsely chop the tomatoes. Peel the onions and garlic; chop finely.

❷ Heat the olive oil in a saucepan, add the onion and garlic and fry for about 3 minutes. Next add the tomato pulp, tomato juice and rosemary. Simmer the vegetables for about 20 minutes without a lid. Season with salt and pepper.

❸ Fry the pine nuts in an ungreased pan until golden brown. Cook the ravioli in plenty of salted water, following the instructions on the packet. Pour away the water and drain thoroughly.

❹ Season the tomato sauce with salt and pepper; put the ravioli in a bowl and add the tomato sauce. Stir well. Sprinkle with pine nuts before serving.

**Serves 4. About 825 kcal per serving**

**1 can chopped tomatoes with juice (800 g/1¾ lb)**

**1 onion**

**1 clove garlic**

**4 tablespoons olive oil**

**1 sprig rosemary**

**salt**

**freshly ground pepper**

**3 tablespoons pine nuts**

**800 g/1¾ lb fresh ravioli (with spinach filling)**

# Fried tomatoes with mint sauce

The lightly mint-flavoured sauce makes a perfect accompaniment to the fried tomatoes. It is excellent with hot spicy dishes, such as meat balls with chilli, because its cool, refreshing taste pleasantly counter-balances the spiciness of the dish.

❶ Cut the plum tomatoes lengthways into slices 1 cm/⅜ in thick. Season with salt and leave to stand for about 15 minutes.

❷ Heat the oil in a pan, add the tomato slices, a few at a time, and fry on both sides until golden brown. Put in a warm place.

❸ For the sauce: pour the yoghurt into large bowl and stir until smooth. Add the remaining ingredients, stir again and season to taste.

❹ Serve the sauce separately from the tomatoes.

**Serves 4. About 119 kcal per serving**

**8 plum tomatoes**

**salt**

**olive oil for cooking**

**500 ml/17 fl oz (2¼ cups) yoghurt**

**1 tablespoon curry powder**

**1 pinch ground cinnamon**

**1 tablespoon chopped fresh mint**

**1 tablespoon lemon juice**

**pepper**

**cayenne pepper**

# Candied tomatoes

This baked sweet-and-sour tomato dish is delicious with crisp roast chicken, and they can both be cooked at the same time in a fan oven. While they both cook, there is plenty of time to clear up the kitchen – useful when guests are expected.

800 g/1¾ lb beef tomatoes

2 slices white bread

1 small container green
   peppercorns in brine

3 tablespoons brown sugar

3 tablespoons white wine-
   vinegar

½ teaspoon dried basil

white pepper from the mill

butter for the mould

❶ Pre-heat the oven to 200°C (400°F), Gas mark 6.

❷ Peel the tomatoes, cut into quarters and remove the seeds. Cut the crusts off the slices of white bread and cut them into large cubes. Remove the peppercorns from the brine and crush with the back of a knife. Reserve the brine.

❸ Put the tomato pieces and diced bread in a bowl and mix well. Add the sugar, vinegar, basil and green peppercorns, and lastly the brine. Stir well. Season with pepper and salt. Taste and season again if necessary.

❹ Butter a baking tin generously and add the tomato mixture. Put on the middle shelf of the oven and cook for 30-40 minutes.

**Serves 4. About 139 kcal per serving**

# Tomato gratin with olives and herbs

Gratiné tomatoes with black olives and herbs are very tasty with a crusty baguette. They are even more delicious served with fried sardines, washed down with a glass of Pinot Bianco.

butter for the mould

16 black olives, stoned (pitted)

1 bunch smooth parsley

4 large beef tomatoes

4 tablespoons oil

4 tablespoons breadcrumbs

1 egg yolks

salt

pepper

½ teaspoon dried basil

❶ Pre-heat the oven to 220°C (425°F), Gas mark 7. Butter a baking tin generously.

❷ Chop the olives and parsley. Cut the top off the tomatoes and carefully remove the pulp using a teaspoon. Chop the tomato pulp. Put the chopped tomato pulp in a bowl and add the oil, olives and parsley. Add the breadcrumbs and egg and mix thoroughly. Season with salt, pepper and basil.

❸ Place the hollowed out tomatoes next to each other in the baking tin and fill with the tomato and olive mixture. Put on the middle shelf of the oven and bake for about 20 minutes.

**Serves 4. About 255 kcal per serving**

# Tomatoes with tofu (bean curd) and basil dumplings

The perfect dish for a hot summer's day – a light, refreshing starter (appetizer) which is quick and easy to prepare.

**❶** Crumble the tofu (bean curd) finely and mix with the curd cheese. Peel the garlic and spring onions (scallions) and chop finely. Wash the basil and pat it dry. Put a few basil leaves aside for the garnish and finely chop the rest. Add the garlic, spring onions (scallions), basil and walnuts to the tofu (bean curd) and cheese mixture and stir well. Leave to stand briefly.

**❷** Wash the tomatoes, remove the stalks, cut into slices and arrange on a dish. Mix together the vinegar, oil, salt, pepper and sugar to make a marinade and pour over the tomatoes. Moisten your hands and roll the prepared mixture into little dumplings. Add them to the tomatoes and garnish with basil leaves.

**Serves 4. About 254 kcal per serving**

150 g/5 oz tofu (bean curd)

100 g/3½ in curd cheese

2 cloves garlic

2 spring onions (scallions)

10–12 leaves of basil

3 tablespoons finely chopped walnuts

700 g/1½ lb sliced firm tomatoes

1 tablespoon balsamic vinegar

5 teaspoons olive oil

salt

freshly ground pepper

½ teaspoon sugar

1 can chopped tomatoes
  (400 g/14 oz)

2 small onions

2 cloves garlic

2 tablespoons olive oil

120 g/5oz (¾ cup) risotto rice

350 ml/12 fl oz (1½ cups) tomato
  juice

150 ml/5 fl oz (⅝ cup) vegetable
  stock (broth)

sugar

salt

pepper

50 g/2 oz (½ cup) grated Parmesan

parsley

butter for the mould

2 cloves garlic

8 tablespoons olive oil

2 tablespoons dried herbs of
  Provence

salt

white pepper from the mill

8 medium tomatoes

# Tomato risotto

This tomato risotto is an ideal accompaniment for meat and liver dishes, and also for fish. For a more seasoned risotto, the vegetable stock (broth) can be replaced with dry white wine.

❶ Drain the tomatoes. Peel the onions and garlic and chop finely. Heat the oil in a large saucepan, add the chopped onion and garlic and fry a little to soften. Add the risotto rice and stir well, using a wooden spoon. Fry briefly.

❷ Little by little add the tomato juice and then the vegetable stock (broth) to the risotto, stirring all the time, while the risotto cooks on a low heat for 20 minutes. Add some water if the risotto needs more liquid.

❸ When the risotto is ready, add the chopped tomatoes. Stir and heat up the risotto again. Season with sugar, salt and pepper. Sprinkle with Parmesan and parsley just before serving.

**Serves 4. About 252 kcal per serving**

# Tomatoes
# à la Provençale

These baked tomatoes seasoned with herbs of Provence conjure up images of sun, sea, sand… and France. Delicious when served with rabbit in mustard sauce and crusty white bread.

❶ Pre-heat the oven to 220°C (425°F), Gas mark 7. Butter a baking tin generously. Peel the garlic.

❷ Add the herbs and pressed garlic to the oil. Season with salt and pepper.

❸ Cut the tomatoes into three, remove the seeds and salt lightly. Place the tomato pieces in the baking tin and pour the herb oil over them.

❹ Put on the middle shelf of the oven and bake for 30 minutes.

**Serves 4. About 221 kcal per serving**

# Fried green tomatoes with béchamel sauce

6 soft green tomatoes (already showing traces of orange)

3 eggs

50 g/2 oz (4 tablespoons) clarified butter

1–2 cups breadcrumbs

salt

pepper

65 g/2½ oz (5 tablespoons) butter

6 tablespoons flour

500 ml/17 fl oz (2¼ cups) milk

nutmeg

Tabasco

1 egg yolk

Green tomatoes do not only play a part in the movie of the same name, they also stand out in this mouth-watering dish, served with a tasty white sauce.

❶ Slice the green tomatoes. Beat the eggs.

❷ Pre-heat the oven to its lowest setting, 80°C (175°F). Heat the clarified butter in a large saucepan.

❸ Dip the tomato slices first in the beaten eggs, then in the breadcrumbs. On a medium heat, carefully fry the breaded tomato slices a few at a time until golden brown. Season with salt and pepper, arrange on a baking sheet lined with kitchen paper and put in the oven to keep warm.

❹ For the sauce: melt the butter in a saucepan and add flour. Stir vigorously with a whisk and slowly add the milk while stirring. Season with salt, pepper, nutmeg and Tabasco. Remove the saucepan from the heat and when it is no longer boiling, stir the egg yolks into the sauce.

❺ Put the tomatoes on individual plates and serve the hot sauce separately.

**Serves 4. About 561 kcal per serving**

# Aubergine and courgette (eggplant and zucchini) rolls with tomato sauce

For this sophisticated recipe a slicing machine makes it easier to cut the aubergines (eggplants) and courgettes (zucchini) into very regular, thin slices. Delicious with hot ciabatta bread and a glass of Italian red wine.

**❶** Slice the aubergines (eggplants) and courgettes (zucchini) lengthways into very thin slices.

**❷** Heat 1 tablespoon of oil in a pan, add the breadcrumbs and fry until golden brown, stirring continuously. Then add the parsley, basil, Parmesan and one of the garlic cloves, stirring well.

**❸** Spread a layer of the herb mixture on the aubergine (eggplant) and courgette (zucchini) slices, roll them up in slices of mozzarella and secure with cocktail sticks.

**❹** Heat 1 tablespoon olive oil in a pan, add the courgette (zucchini) and aubergine (eggplant) rolls and fry for 10 minutes; keep in a warm place.

**❺** For the tomato sauce: peel the onion and cloves of garlic and chop finely. Heat 1 tablespoon of olive oil in a saucepan, add the onion and garlic and sweat until transparent. Drain the tomatoes, crush with a fork and add to the onion and garlic. Pour in the red wine. Bring to the boil and simmer until cooked. Season with salt, pepper and chilli powder.

**❻** Put the aubergine (eggplant) and courgette (zucchini) rolls in the tomato sauce, cover and allow to stand for about 10 minutes. Arrange the rolls on four plates with the tomato sauce.

**Serves 4. About 388 kcal per serving**

2 aubergines (eggplants)

2 courgettes (zucchini)

200 g/7 oz mozzarella

4 tablespoons olive oil

3 tablespoons breadcrumbs

1 bunch parsley, finely chopped

1 bunch basil, finely chopped

2 cloves garlic, finely chopped

40 g/1½ oz (⅜ cup) freshly grated Parmesan

salt

freshly ground pepper

1 onion

1 can chopped tomatoes (800 g/1¾ lb)

4 tablespoons red wine

chilli powder

# Mashed potato gratin with tomato sauce

This mashed potato gratin served with tomato sauce is a delicious, light vegetarian dish which is just as enjoyable as many meat and fish dishes.

**❶** Boil unpeeled potatoes for about 25 minutes until soft. Pre-heat the oven to 220°C (425°F), Gas mark 7.

**❷** Peel the boiled potatoes, put in a bowl and mash with a fork. Add the Parmesan, butter, milk and egg. Purée this mixture in a blender until it is smooth and homogenous. If it seems too dry, add some milk. Season the mash with salt, pepper and nutmeg.

**❸** Put the mashed potato in four small moulds and cook on the middle shelf of the oven for 15 –20 minutes until golden brown.

**❹** For the tomato sauce: cut the tomatoes into four and dice finely. Peel the shallots and cloves of garlic, chop finely.

**❺** Heat the oil in a saucepan, add the chopped garlic and shallots and fry. Add the diced tomatoes and tomato ketchup; season with herbs, a little sugar, salt and pepper. Simmer the tomato sauce for about 10 minutes. Remove the rosemary.

**❻** Serve the tomato sauce hot with the mashed potato gratin.

**Serves 4. About 379 kcal per serving**

1 kg/2¼ lb potatoes, cooked floury

1 tablespoon grated Parmesan

60 g/2 oz (4 tablespoons) butter

250 ml/8 fl oz (1 cup) milk

1 egg

nutmeg

pepper

salt

600 g/1¼ lb ripe tomatoes

2 shallots

1 clove garlic

oil for the pan

1 teaspoon tomato ketchup

½ teaspoon dried Italian herbs

1 small sprig rosemary

sugar

# Grilled avocados with tomato and bread stuffing

As well as being delicious served cold in salad or in a guacamole dip for spicy crisps, avocados are also excellent in hot dishes such as this vegetable gratin with tomatoes. Their flavour combines beautifully with the sweet-and-sour taste of the tomatoes.

1 can chopped tomatoes (400 g/14 oz)

4 shallots

2 slices coriander bread

1 bunch of basil

5 tablespoons vegetable oil

salt

white pepper

1 teaspoon balsamic vinegar

2 avocados

juice of 1 lemon

2 tablespoons breadcrumbs

1 tablespoon grated Parmesan

❶ Drain the tomato pieces, peel the shallots and cut into thin rings. Remove the crusts from the coriander bread and cut into 1 cm/⅜ in cubes. Chop up the basil.

❷ Heat 2 tablespoons of oil in a pan, add the bread cubes and fry on all sides. Pour the bread cubes with the fat into a large bowl. Add the tomato pieces, onion rings and basil and stir well. Season with salt, pepper and vinegar.

❸ Pre-heat the oven to 220°C (425°F), Gas mark 7.

❹ Cut the avocados in half lengthways, remove the stone (seed) and scoop out some of the flesh with a tablespoon. Dice the scooped-out flesh and immediately sprinkle it and the avocado halves with lemon juice. Add the diced avocado flesh to the bread mixture and stir it in.

❺ Fill the avocado halves with the bread mixture. Mix the breadcrumbs and Parmesan with the rest of the oil and pour over the stuffing.

❻ Put the avocados next to each other in a gratin dish. Cook on the middle shelf of the oven for about 20 minutes until brown.

**Serves 4. About 446 kcal per serving**

# Stuffed tomatoes with rice and sultanas (golden raisins)

These tomatoes stuffed with rice and sultanas (golden raisins) and other tasty ingredients including almonds, curry powder and cinnamon are delicious with most lamb dishes.

2 shallots

8 beef tomatoes

150 g/5 oz (¾ cup) rice

2 teaspoons chopped almonds

50 g/2 oz (⅓ cup) sultanas (golden raisins)

ground cinnamon

curry powder

salt

pepper

4 tablespoons tomato ketchup

8 tablespoons sunflower oil

❶ Peel and chop the shallots. Cut the tops off the tomatoes and carefully remove the tomato pulp using a teaspoon.

❷ Chop the tomato pulp finely and put in a bowl. Add the uncooked rice, chopped shallots, chopped almonds and sultanas (golden raisins). Stir well and sprinkle lightly with cinnamon and curry powder. Season with salt and pepper. Stir thoroughly again.

❸ Put the hollowed-out tomatoes next to each other in a large saucepan and fill with the tomato and rice stuffing. Mix the oil and tomato ketchup and pour over the tomatoes. Carefully fill the saucepan with water to reach halfway up the tomatoes.

❹ Cover the saucepan, bring to the boil and simmer gently for about 30 minutes. Remove the stuffed tomatoes from the saucepan with a perforated spoon.

**Serves 4. About 404 kcal per serving**

# Flans and baked dishes

Tomato combined with cheese is a common ingredient of many baked vegetable dishes, such as Tomato and couscous bake (page 96) and Aubergine (eggplant) stuffed with tuna and cherry tomatoes (page 94). Then there is the whole range of pizzas, quiches and flans, including Pizza Margherita (page 92), Tomato quiche with rocket (page 87) and Tomato flan with zucchini (page 85).

# Tomato and goat's cheese bread gratin

This simple little dish can also be prepared with mild sheep's milk cheese. Instead of walnuts and basil, you can sprinkle the gratin with pine nuts and thyme or oregano, fresh or dried.

5 large tomatoes

200 g/7 oz goat's cheese

herb salt

freshly ground pepper

½ baguette

7 tablespoons olive oil

35 g/1½ oz (⅜ cup) coarsely chopped walnut kernels

1 small bunch basil, finely chopped

❶ Slice the tomatoes and goat's cheese. Sprinkle herb salt and a little freshly ground pepper on the tomato slices. Cut the baguette diagonally into 12 slices.

❷ Pre-heat the oven to 200°C (400°F), Gas mark 6. Heat 4 tablespoons of olive oil in a pan. Fry the baguette slices briefly on both sides and leave to cool slightly.

❸ Grease a gratin dish with 1 tablespoon of oil. Arrange the slices of bread, tomatoes and cheese in alternate layers in the gratin dish. Pour the rest of the olive oil over the gratin. Bake in the oven for about 10 minutes.

❹ Shortly before the gratin is ready to come out of the oven, sprinkle with walnuts and basil. Serve hot.

**Serves 4. About 433 kcal per serving**

# Tomato and herb gratin with sheep's milk cheese

This tomato and sheep's milk cheese gratin, served with Tuscan white bread or potatoes in their skins makes a delicious, light meal.

4 tablespoons oil

1 kg/2¼ lb tomatoes

herb salt

freshly ground pepper

2 cloves garlic

2 tablespoons basil, finely chopped

2 tablespoons thyme, finely chopped

2 tablespoons marjoram, finely chopped

250 g/9 oz mild sheep's cheese

❶ Pre-heat the oven to 220°C (425°F), Gas mark 7. Grease a gratin dish with 1 tablespoon of oil. Cut the tomatoes in two and put in the gratin dish with the cut surfaces upwards. Season with salt and pepper.

❷ Peel the garlic cloves. Chop finely; add ½ tablespoon each of thyme and marjoram, 1 tablespoon basil, and the rest of the olive oil. Stir well. Coat the cut surfaces of the tomatoes with this oil and herb mixture.

❸ Cut the sheep's milk cheese into thin slices and put on top of the tomatoes. Bake in the pre-heated oven for about 15 minutes. Sprinkle with the rest of the herbs before serving.

**Serves 4. About 285 kcal per serving**

# Tomato flan with herbs

A particularly tasty flan with a base made from wholemeal (whole wheat) flour. To save time, the dough can be prepared the previous day and kept in the refrigerator, wrapped in clingfilm.

120 g/5 oz (⅝ cup) chilled butter

175 g/6 oz (2 cups) flour

¼ teaspoon salt

¼ teaspoon chopped thyme

fat for the mould

flour for the work surface


For the topping:

500 g/18 oz large tomatoes

150 g/5 oz Gruyère cheese

salt

freshly ground pepper

1 tablespoon chopped fresh basil

1 tablespoon chopped fresh marjoram

20 g/¾ oz (¼ cup) freshly grated Parmesan

25 g/1 oz (2 tablespoons) melted butter

❶ To make the dough: cut the butter into small pieces and add to the flour, salt and thyme on the work surface. Add 3–5 tablespoons of ice-cold water and quickly knead to make a dough. Shape into a ball, wrap in clingfilm and put in the refrigerator for 30 minutes.

❷ Slice the tomatoes and cheese for the filling. Sprinkle the tomatoes with salt and leave to drain on a cake rack for about 30 minutes.

❸ Pre-heat the oven to 200°C (400°F), Gas mark 6. Grease a spring-mould 22 cm/8½ in in diameter. On a lightly floured work surface, roll out two-thirds of the dough to the size of the spring-mould. Line the spring-mould with it. Roll out the rest of the dough to line the sides of the mould. Prick the base several times with a fork. Bake in the oven for about 15 minutes.

❹ Arrange the cheese and tomato slices on the base. Season with freshly ground pepper on top. Sprinkle basil, marjoram and Parmesan on the cheese and tomatoes slices. Pour some melted butter on top . Bake for 20–25 minutes at 180°C (350°F), Gas mark 4. Serve hot.

**Serves 4. About 630 kcal per serving**

# Tomato flan with courgettes (zucchini)

What distinguishes the tomato quiche from a pizza is the sour cream with beaten eggs and herbs which is poured over the vegetables. So as an alternative you can make a delicious pizza by coating the base with tomato sauce, arranging the vegetables on it and sprinkling the top with oregano, grated cheese and a little olive oil.

**1** Pre-heat the oven to 220°C (425°F), Gas mark 7. Grease a baking-tin.

**2** Crumble the yeast into 150 ml/4 fl oz (⅝ cup) lukewarm water and stir well. Sift the flour over a bowl and add the yeast with the water, melted butter and a pinch of salt. Stir to make a smooth mixture. Cover the bowl with a tea towel. Leave to rise in a warm place for about 15 minutes.

**3** Halve the tomatoes, remove the seeds and slice. Clean and wash the courgettes (zucchini) and slice.

**4** Roll out the yeast dough on a floured work surface and transfer to the baking tin. Press the dough down, pull into shape and form an edge. Prick the base with a fork.

**5** Arrange the tomato and courgette (zucchini) slices on the base. Season with salt and sprinkle with grated cheese.

**6** Stir the sour cream until smooth and add the beaten eggs and herbs. Stir again. Pour this mixture over the vegetables. Put on the bottom shelf of the oven and bake for 30–40 minutes. Serve hot.

**Serves 4. About 649 kcal per serving**

---

**fat for the baking sheet**

**10 g (2 teaspoons) fresh yeast or 5 g (1 teaspoon) dried yeast**

**250 g/9 oz (2¼ cups) flour**

**75 g/3 oz (6 tablespoons) melted butter**

**salt**

**500 g/18 oz medium tomatoes**

**500 g/18 oz courgettes (zucchini)**

**flour for the work surface**

**100 g/3½ oz (1 cup) grated Gruyère cheese,**

**100 ml/3½ oz (scant ½ cup) sour cream**

**2 eggs**

**1 tablespoon dried herbs of Provence**

# Tomato quiche
# with rocket

The base of this tomato, onion, rocket, salami and ham quiche is made with a yeast dough. For the best results all the ingredients must be at room temperature, including the egg. All the ingredients should therefore be taken out of the refrigerator in good time.

❶ To make the dough: sift the flour into a bowl and make a hollow in the centre. Sprinkle in the yeast and sugar and pour in the lukewarm milk. Mix, adding the flour little by little from the edges. Stand for about 10 minutes in a warm place.

❷ Add 100 g/3½ oz (½ cup) butter at room temperature, ½ teaspoon salt and the egg. Work into a dough by hand or using the kneading hook of the mixer. Sprinkle flour on the dough, cover the bowl with a tea towel and put in a warm place. The dough can be worked again when it has doubled in size. Knead the dough vigorously after it has risen. Butter a quiche dish generously.

❸ Roll out the dough about 1 cm (⅜ in) thick and line the quiche dish. Prick the base with a fork. Pour 60 g/2 oz (4 tablespoons) melted butter over the base. Leave to rise in a very cool oven, 50°C/120°F, for 20–30 minutes. Remove, then pre-heat the oven to 200°C (400°F), Gas mark 6.

❹ Peel the onions and divide into rings. Cut the tomatoes into four, remove the seeds and chop coarsely. Tear the rocket into bite-sized pieces and cut the salami and boiled ham into strips.

❺ Put the sour cream and quark in bowl and stir into a smooth mixture. Beat in the egg yolk. Season with salt and pepper. Pour the sour cream mixture onto the base.

❻ Heat the rest of the butter in a pan, add the onion rings, fry until transparent and remove. Fry the tomatoes briefly in the same butter and season with salt and pepper. Arrange the onion rings and tomato pieces in the sour cream mixture. Add the strips of salami and ham. Garnish with rocket. Bake in the oven for about 30 minutes. Serve hot or cold.

**Serves 4. About 998 kcal per serving**

350 g/12 oz (3¼ cups) flour

5 g (1 teaspoon) dried yeast

½ teaspoon sugar

150 ml/5 fl oz (⅝ cup) milk, lukewarm

200 g/7 oz (1 cup) butter

salt

1 egg

butter for the mould

2 red onions

3 beef tomatoes

½ bunch rocket

50 g/2 oz salami

50 g/2 oz cooked ham

100 ml/3½ oz (scant ½ cup) sour cream

100 g/3½ oz quark

2 egg yolks

pepper

# Tomato torte

An important word of advice – use sour cream rather than cream!
It enhances the taste of a tomato torte, whether served hot or cold.

**❶** Pre-heat the oven to 190°C (375°F), Gas mark 5. Butter a spring-mould 26 cm/10¼ in in diameter) generously.

**❷** Mix flour, a pinch of salt, porridge (rolled) oats, butter and egg yolk with 5–6 tablespoons water and knead into a dough. Roll out the dough on a lightly floured work surface and line the base and sides of the spring-mould with it. Bake the case in the bottom part of the oven for about 15 minutes.

**❸** Cut the streaky bacon into thin strips, wash the green pepper and dice finely. Cut the tomatoes into four, remove the seeds and cut each quarter into half again. Grate the Parmesan coarsely. Put all the prepared ingredients in the pastry case.

**❹** Stir the sour cream until smooth. Whisk in the eggs and corn flour (corn starch) and season with salt and cayenne pepper. Add the basil to the sour cream mixture and pour over the ingredients. Bake the tomato torte in the oven for 30–40 minutes until ready. Serve hot or cold.

**Serves 4. About 1,052 kcal per serving**

butter for the mould

125 g/5 oz (1¼ cups) flour

salt

125 g/5 oz (1½ cups) fine porridge (rolled) oats

125 g/5 oz (⅝ cup) butter

1 egg yolks

flour for the work surface

125 g/5 oz streaky bacon

1 green pepper

3 medium tomatoes

125 g/5 oz Parmesan in the piece

250 g/9 oz sour cream

3 eggs

2 tablespoons cornflour (corn starch)

cayenne pepper

1 handful basil leaves

# Small herb tartlets with tomato sauce

The secret of these tasty herb tartlets lies in the dough which is made from boiled potatoes, butter, eggs, spices and herbs. Even better is that this sophisticated flan looks much more complicated to make than it really is!

**❶** Cook the potatoes in their skins for about 25 minutes. Peel the boiled potatoes and mash with a fork.

**❷** Bring 200 ml/7 fl oz (⅞ cup) water to the boil in a saucepan with the butter and remove from the heat. Add the porridge (rolled) oats and eggs little by little. Bring back to the boil while stirring and continue until the mixture detaches itself from the sides of the pan. Add the potato purée. Season with salt, pepper and herbs. Put the dough in the refrigerator and leave to rest.

**❸** Pre-heat the oven to 200°C (400°F), Gas mark 6. Butter a baking sheet generously.

**❹** To make the tomato sauce: put the chopped tomatoes and juice in a saucepan and bring to the boil. Simmer without a lid for about 20 minutes. Peel the clove of garlic and the onion. Chop finely and add to the tomato sauce. Add the basil and season to taste with salt and pepper. Leave the sauce to cool down.

**❺** Form the dough mixture into about 18 tartlets and put on the baking sheet. Bake for about 15 minutes on the middle shelf of the oven until golden brown. Serve hot with the cold tomato sauce.

**Serves 4. About 372 kcal per serving**

250 g/9 oz potatoes, cooked floury

60 g/2 oz (4 tablespoons) butter

120 g/4 oz porridge (rolled) oats

3 eggs

salt

pepper

4 tablespoons dried Italian herbs

butter for the baking sheet

1 can chopped tomatoes (400 g/14 oz)

250 ml/8 fl oz (1 cup) tomato juice

1 clove garlic

1 onion

1 handful chopped basil leaves

# Tomato and minced (ground) meat loaf

This dish is an excellent source of protein because of the minced (ground) meat and cheese. It is delicious served with a refreshing salad and white bread, and can be eaten hot or cold.

3 small onions

1 teaspoon capers

500 g/18 oz minced (ground) meat

1 teaspoon tomato purée

½ teaspoon chopped oregano

salt

freshly ground pepper

paprika pepper

1 egg

2 tablespoons breadcrumbs

fat for the mould

750 g/1¾ lb large tomatoes

1 bunch basil

250 g/9 oz small mozzarella-rolls

250 g/9 oz grated Emmenthal cheese

❶ Pre-heat the oven to 220°C (425°F), Gas mark 7. Peel the onions and chop finely. Do the same with the capers. Mix the minced (ground) meat, onions, capers, tomato pulp, spices, egg and breadcrumbs to make a paste. Grease a flan mould 26 cm/10¼ in in diameter and add the minced (ground) meat mixture. Smooth the top.

❷ Cut the tomatoes in two and hollow out. Put one basil leaf and one drained mozzarella ball in each tomato half. Arrange the tomatoes in a circle round the edge of the flan mould, cut side downwards, and press lightly into the minced (ground) meat mixture. Season with salt and pepper.

❸ Sprinkle the minced (ground) meat mixture with the grated cheese and bake in the pre-heated oven on the second-bottom shelf for about 30 minutes. It can be served hot or cold.

**Serves 4. About 740 kcal per serving**

# Pasta loaf with basil and tomato sauce

This pasta loaf looks particularly pretty when prepared with green and white sheets of lasagne. Alternate the green and white sheets to create a stripy effect.

**❶** Soak the the sheets of lasagne pasta in cold water for 50–60 minutes. Drain the mozzarella and cut into cubes. Cut the ham into strips.

**❷** For the sauce: peel the onion and the clove of garlic. Chop the onion finely and press the garlic. Heat the oil in a saucepan, add the onion and garlic and fry until transparent. Stir in the tomato pulp and sweat lightly. Add flour, stir in, then add the beef stock (broth). Bring the sauce to the boil and simmer over a low heat for 5 minutes.

**❸** Pour the sauce through a fine sieve and season with sugar, salt and pepper. Chop the basil finely and stir it into the sauce. Use half the sauce for the pasta loaf and reserve the rest in a warm place.

**❹** Pre-heat the oven to 160°C (325°F), Gas mark 3. Line a flan tin with two-thirds of the drained sheets of lasagne and put the rest to one side. Fill with layers of spiral noodles, mozzarella, ham and Parmesan. Pour tomato sauce over each layer. Finally, press the filling down a little and dot with flakes of butter. Use the remaining sheets of lasagne to cover the pasta loaf. Coat the top with egg yolk.

**❺** Bake the pasta loaf in the oven for about 45 minutes. Leave to cool down in the mould for 10 minutes, then cut into slices. Serve with the rest of the tomato sauce.

**Serves 4. About 800 kcal per serving**

300 g/10 oz sheets of lasagne

250 g/8 oz mozzarella

150 g/5 oz cooked ham

1 onion

1 clove garlic

1 tablespoon olive oil

150 g/5 oz tomato purée

30 g/1 oz (¼ cup) flour

750 ml/1¼ pints (3½ cups) beef stock (broth)

1 pinch sugar

salt

freshly ground pepper

1 bunch basil

300 g/10 oz pasta twirls

40 g/1½ oz (⅜ cup) freshly grated Parmesan

30 g/1 oz (2 tablespoons) butter

1 egg yolks

# Pizza Margherita

This famous pizza was created in honour of Queen Margherita of Italy, and it displays the three colours of the Italian flag: green basil, white mozzarella and red tomatoes.

**20 g/¾ oz yeast**
**300 g/11 oz flour**
**1 pinch salt**
**olive oil for the baking sheet**
**2 tablespoons olive oil**
**flour for the work surface**

for the topping:
**500 g/18 oz fresh tomatoes**
**250 g/9 oz mozzarella**
**1 small bunch basil**
**salt**
**ground white pepper**
**6 tablespoons olive oil**

❶ To make the dough: crumble the yeast which should be at room temperature) in a cup, add 2 tablespoons lukewarm water and stir. Sift the flour into a large bowl, add salt and make a well in the centre. Pour in the yeast mixture and sprinkle a little flour on top. Put in a warm place to rise until it has doubled in size.

❷ Add 125 ml/4 fl oz (½ cup) of lukewarm water to the risen dough and work vigorously by hand or with the dough hook of the mixer. Knead vigorously until the dough becomes smooth with an elastic consistency. Shape into a ball, cover and put in a warm place to rise until it has doubled in height.

❸ Pre-heat the oven to 220°C (425°F), Gas mark 7. Grease a baking sheet with olive oil. On it, knead the dough again vigorously but briefly to work in the olive oil. Roll out flat on a lightly floured work surface and form a slightly raised edge.

❹ For the topping: peel the tomatoes, cut them into quarters and remove the seeds. Cut the tomato quarters into strips and arrange on the pizza base. Now add the thinly sliced mozzarella and basil leaves. Season with salt and pepper and sprinkle with olive oil. Bake the pizza on the bottom shelf of the oven for about 30 minutes.

**Serves 4. About 574 kcal per serving**

# Aubergine (eggplant) stuffed with tuna and cherry tomatoes

400 g/14 oz beef tomatoes

½ bunch parsley

1 handful leaves of basil

2 shallots

2 cloves garlic

4 tablespoons sunflower oil

salt

pepper

3 small aubergines (eggplants)

120 g/4 oz cherry tomatoes

oil for the mould

150 g/5 oz tuna fish, natural, without oil

3 tablespoons porridge (rolled) oats

60 g/2 oz Parmesan

1 teaspoon lemon juice

1 egg

A delicious Mediterranean dish: aubergines (eggplants) stuffed with tomatoes, herbs and tuna fish, topped with Parmesan. Excellent with a glass of white wine such as Orvieto.

❶ Cut the tomatoes into quarters, remove the seeds and dice. Chop the parsley and basil. Peel the shallots and garlic, then chop them finely. Heat 2 tablespoons of oil in a saucepan. Fry the shallots and garlic. Next add the diced tomatoes and herbs. Season with salt and pepper. Add 3 tablespoons of water and simmer over a low heat for about 30 minutes. Stir from time to time.

❷ Remove the stalks from the aubergines (eggplants) and cut in half lengthways. Hollow out carefully using a tablespoon and cut the pulp into cubes. Sprinkle the cubes and the hollowed-out aubergines (eggplants) with a little salt. Cut the cherry tomatoes into slices.

❸ Pre-heat the oven to 200°C (400°F), Gas mark 6. Grease a large roasting tin generously with oil.

❹ Drain the tuna fish and pick the tuna apart with a fork. Heat 2 tablespoons of oil in a large frying pan and fry the tuna briefly. Add the tomato mixture, stir and season with salt and pepper.

❺ Dry the aubergine (eggplant) halves and diced pulp with kitchen paper. Sprinkle 1½ tablespoons of rolled oats over the aubergine (eggplant) halves and fill with the diced bouillon pulp and tuna and tomato mixture. Sprinkle half the Parmesan on top. Garnish with the cherry tomatoes.

❻ Put the stuffed aubergines (eggplants) in the roasting tin. Mix the remaining rolled oats and Parmesan, add the lemon juice and egg and stir well. Season with salt and pepper and pour over the aubergines (eggplants). Put the roasting tin on the middle shelf of the oven and bake for about 45 minutes.

**Serves 4. About 448 kcal per serving**

# Tomato and Gouda bake

Various kinds of cheese can be used for this recipe. Emmenthal or Gruyère may replace the Gouda, and Pecorino is an alternative to the Parmesan.

❶ Pre-heat the oven to 220°C (425°F), Gas mark 7. Grease a soufflé dish generously with butter. Grate the Gouda and Parmesan. Peel the tomatoes and cut into slices.

❷ Pour the sour cream into a bowl and stir until smooth. Add the grated cheese and season with salt and pepper.

❸ Line the bottom of the soufflé dish with the tomato slices. Season with salt and pepper. Pour a layer of the sour cream mixture over the tomatoes and continue alternating layers of tomatoes and sour cream, ending with the sour cream mixture.

❹ Put on the middle shelf of the oven and bake for 20–30 minutes.

**Serves 4. About 395 kcal per serving**

**butter for the mould**

**100 g/3½ oz mature Gouda**

**50 g/2 oz Parmesan**

**800 g/1¾ lb beef tomatoes**

**200 ml/7 fl oz (7/8 cup) sour cream**

**salt**

**pepper**

# Tomato soufflé with creamy quark

The creamy quark gives this tomato soufflé a creamy texture while the Emmenthal or Gruyère cheese and Parmesan add a pleasantly tangy taste. It is delicious served with toasted white bread, sprinkled with garlic oil.

❶ Grate the mountain cheese. Beat the egg whites until they form stiff peaks. Generously butter a soufflé dish. Cut the tomatoes into quarters and remove the seeds.

❷ Pre-heat the oven to 220°C (425°F), Gas mark 7. Pour the creamy quark into a bowl and stir until smooth. Add the egg yolk and whisk vigorously. Stir in the grated mountain cheese and season with nutmeg, salt and pepper. Fold the stiffly beaten egg whites carefully into the quark.

❸ Pour the quark mixture into the soufflé dish and smooth the top. Press the tomato quarters into the creamy mixture. Season with salt and pepper and sprinkle with basil and Parmesan.

❹ Put the tomato soufflé on the middle shelf of the oven and bake for about 30 minutes.

**Serves 4. About 458 kcal per serving**

**100 g/3½ oz Emmenthal or Gruyère**

**4 egg white**

**butter for the mould**

**10 medium tomatoes**

**500 g/18 oz cream quark**

**4 egg yolks**

**1 pinch nutmeg**

**salt**

**white pepper from the mill**

**1 tablespoon chopped basil**

**50 g/2 oz (½ cup) grated Parmesan**

# Tomato and couscous bake

Couscous dishes are very popular in North African countries such as Tunisia. It may be served with vegetables, poultry and other meats.

250 g/9 oz couscous

butter for the mould

4 large beef tomatoes

2 tablespoons oil

1 tablespoon parsley, chopped

1 bay leaf

salt

pepper

100 g/3½ oz (1 cup) grated
   Emmenthal cheese

❶ Put the couscous in a bowl and pour a little hot water over it – the couscous must be moist but not sitting in water. Cover the bowl with a large lid or aluminium foil and leave to soak for a few minutes.

❷ Pre-heat the oven to 220°C (425°F), Gas mark 7. Butter a soufflé dish generously.

❸ Cut the tomatoes into quarters, remove the seeds and chop coarsely. Heat the oil in a large pan and add the chopped tomatoes, parsley and bay leaves; season generously with salt and pepper. Cover and simmer over a low heat for about 30 minutes until the mixture has reduced to make a thick sauce. Stir now and again.

❹ Put a layer of couscous at the bottom of the soufflé dish with a layer of tomato purée on top. Follow with a layer of grated cheese, another layer of couscous and finally a layer of tomato purée. Sprinkle with grated cheese. Bake the soufflé for about 20 minutes in the oven.

**Serves 4. About 179 kcal per serving**

# Tomato and mozzarella gratin

An exquisitely light gratin made of overlapping slices of tomato and mozzarella which can easily be prepared in larger quantities if necessary. Serve with French bread and a mixed salad.

❶ Drain the mozzarella and slice. Cut the tomatoes into slices. Peel the clove of garlic and chop finely. Coarsely chop the basil and parsley.

❷ Break the crispbread into small pieces, put in a liquidizer and turn into crumbs. Work the herb butter (at room temperature) into the bread crumbs.

❸ Pre-heat the oven to 200°C (400°F), Gas mark 6. Butter a gratin dish generously.

❹ Arrange a layer of overlapping slices of tomatoes at the bottom and season with salt, pepper, garlic and herbs; follow by a layer of mozzarella; season with salt and pepper. Continue until all the tomatoes and mozzarella have been used up. Finish off the gratin with a layer of the bread crumbs and herb butter mixture.

❺ Bake the gratin in the oven for about 15 minutes.

**Serves 4. About 449 kcal per serving**

**2 packs mozzarella (200 g/7 oz each)**

**800 g/1¾ lb medium tomatoes**

**1 clove garlic**

**½ bunch basil**

**½ bunch smooth parsley**

**3 slices crispbread**

**60 g/2 oz (4 tablespoons) herb butter**

**butter for the mould**

**salt**

**pepper**

**½ teaspoon dried Italian herbs**

# Tomatoes stuffed with onions

The onion is the most versatile of vegetables. This dish combining onions, tomatoes, garlic, capers and olives will add a festive note to any table.

❶ Peel the onions and chop finely. Heat the oil in a pan. Add the onions and fry. Add the porridge (rolled) oats and stir well. Put the onion mixture in a warm place.

❷ Peel the cloves of garlic and chop up with the capers and olives. Add to the onion mixture and season with oregano, salt and pepper.

❸ Pre-heat the oven to 220°C (425°F), Gas mark 7. Butter a large gratin dish generously.

❹ Cut the tops off the tomatoes and carefully scoop out the pulp using a teaspoon. Sprinkle the scooped out tomatoes lightly with salt and leave them to stand for about 10 minutes. Stuff the tomatoes with a generous amount of the onion mixture, which can be higher than the edges of the scooped out tomatoes. Replace the lids. Put the stuffed tomatoes next to each other in the gratin dish and bake on the middle shelf of the oven for about 30 minutes.

**Serves 4. About 269 kcal per serving**

300 g/11 oz onions

5 tablespoons oil

70 g/3 oz (1 cup) porridge (rolled) oats

2 cloves garlic

20 g/¾ oz capers

50 g/2 oz green olives stuffed with pimento

oregano

salt

pepper

butter for the mould

800 g/1¾ lb medium tomatoes

# Fish and meat

The tomato makes a valuable addition to a festive menu or a sophisticated meal for two because of its great versatility. Prawn (shrimp) with tomato sauce (page 115), Zander with caper and tomato sauce (page 102) and Pork chops on a bed of tomatoes and apple (page 122) are just a few examples. These exquisite dishes have the added advantage of being quick and easy to prepare.

# Squid rings in a tomato cream sauce

Enjoyed with a glass of white wine, these squid rings in a tomato and cream sauce conjure up delightful images of Greece.

800 g/1¾ lb squid rings, frozen

juice of 1 lemon

½ bunch chervil

5 beef tomatoes

250 ml/8 fl oz (1 cup) white wine

2 tablespoons oil

salt

lemon pepper

1 tablespoon crème fraîche

❶ Defrost the squid rings, rinse and wipe dry with kitchen paper. Sprinkle with lemon juice. Chop the chervil.

❷ Peel the tomatoes, cut into quarters and remove the seeds. Chop the tomato pieces finely and purée in the liquidizer on high speed.

❸ Heat the oil in a pan, fry the squid and season with salt and pepper. Remove from the pan. Add the tomato purée and crème fraîche to the pan, bring to the boil gently and season with salt and pepper. Arrange the cuttlefish rings on a dish with the tomato and cream sauce and sprinkle with chervil just before serving.

**Serves 4. About 321 kcal per serving**

# Zander with caper and tomato sauce

Zander or pikeperch is delicious served just with melted butter, but it is even better with the accompaniment of this caper and tomato sauce.

800 g/1¾ lb medium tomatoes

1 clove garlic

1 tablespoon capers

1 bunch smooth parsley

7 tablespoons oil

1 bay leaf

800 g/1¾ lb zander fillets

salt

pepper

❶ Peel the tomatoes, cut into quarters and remove the seeds. Chop up the tomato quarters. Peel the clove of garlic and finely chop the capers and parsley.

❷ Pour 4 tablespoons oil in a large dish and stir in the parsley. Add the bay leaves and fish. Coat the fish completely with the marinade. Cover the dish with aluminium foil and put in the refrigerator for about 1 hour 30 minutes.

❸ Heat the remaining oil in a large pan. Add the capers, pressed garlic and chopped tomatoes and stir. Season with salt and pepper and bring to the boil on a low flame.

❹ Heat a non-stick pan and add the zander and its marinade, but without the bay leaves. Salt the fish and fry for 5–7 minutes on each side.

❺ Arrange the zander fillets on four plates, pour over the sauce and sprinkle with freshly ground pepper.

**Serves 4. About 384 kcal per serving**

# Redfish fillets with tomato and herb topping

750 g/1¾ lb small, ripe tomatoes

800 g/1¾ lb redfish fillets

salt

fat for the mould

5 teaspoons pesto (Italian basil paste)

freshly ground pepper

For the herb coating:

1 onion

2 cloves garlic

30 g/1 oz (2 tablespoons) clarified butter

1 bunch smooth parsley, finely chopped

½ bunch thyme, finely chopped

½ bunch basil, finely chopped

1 teaspoon chopped rosemary

30 g breadcrumbs

2 teaspoons capers

1 tablespoon mustard

2 tablespoons olive oil

salt

freshly ground pepper

Redfish is also known as the Norway haddock, and cod or haddock fillets may be used instead. The pesto may be bought, or home-made as follows. Crush the leaves of a large bunch of basil with 2 tablespoons of pine nuts, 3 cloves of garlic and a pinch of salt in mortar. Stir in 125 ml/4 fl oz (½ cup) olive oil and 50 g/2 oz (½ cup) grated Parmesan. Pour into a screw-top jar and store in the refrigerator.

❶ Pre-heat the oven to 200°C (400°F), Gas mark 6. To make the crusty herb topping: peel the onion and garlic cloves and chop finely. Heat the clarified butter and sweat the chopped garlic and onion until transparent. Remove from the heat and stir in the herbs, breadcrumbs, capers, mustard and olive oil. Season with salt and pepper.

❷ Cut the tomatoes into slices. Wash the fish fillets, wipe them dry, season with salt and cut into portion-sized pieces.

❸ Grease an oven-proof dish and arrange the fish portions in it. Coat lightly with pesto and cover with the tomato slices. Season with salt and freshly ground pepper. Cover the tomato slices with the herb mixture.

❹ Bake the fish fillet on the second shelf of the oven for about 25 minutes.

**Serves 4. About 438 kcal per serving**

# Sole with leeks and tomatoes

Leeks and tomatoes are a perfect accompaniment to any fish dish – fillets of pollack, cod or salmon, or even fish fingers. So if you decide that sole is too expensive, it can always be replaced with another kind of fish.

**❶** Peel the tomatoes, cut them into quarters and remove the seeds. Chop the tomato quarters into small cubes. Peel the onions and wash and clean the leeks. Cut both into thin rings.

**❷** Heat the oil in a pan and fry the onion and leek rings. Add the diced tomatoes and season with salt and pepper. Cook the leek and tomato mixture for about 10 minutes over low heat. Stir in the basil. Put the vegetable mixture in a warm place.

**❸** Remove the skin from the gutted soles and cut off the heads diagonally. Cut off the fins using scissors. Heat the clarified butter in a large pan, add the fillets of sole and fry on both sides until golden brown. Season with salt and pepper.

**❹** Arrange the fish fillets on a serving dish and garnish with the leek and tomato mixture.

**Serves 4. About 377 kcal per serving**

**500 g/18 oz beef tomatoes**

**2 red onions**

**2 small leeks**

**2 tablespoons oil**

**salt**

**pepper**

**1 handful leaves of basil**

**1 kg/2¼ lb sole**

**30 g/1 oz (2 tablespoons) clarified butter**

# Cod fillet in tomato and tarragon sauce with peas

The fish in this low-calorie protein-rich, dish can be replaced by salmon fillet or rose fish. It is delicious served with long grain rice, cooked *al dente*, and dry white wine.

600 g/1¼ lb cod fillets

herb salt

freshly ground pepper

4 small tomatoes

1 large shallot

25 g/1 oz (2 tablespoons) butter

1 small bunch dill, chopped

100 ml/4 fl oz (½ cup) dry white wine

200 ml/8 fl oz (½ cup) tomato sauce (see page 126, or use a commercial product)

1 small bunch tarragon, finely chopped

15 g/1 oz (1 tablespoon) chilled butter pieces

500 g/18 oz peas

salt

❶ Set the oven to a very low heat, 80°C/175°F. Rinse the cod fillet, wipe dry and cut into portion-size pieces. Season with herb salt and pepper. Cut the tomatoes into quarters, remove the seeds and cut into strips. Peel the shallots and chop finely.

❷ Butter a saucepan. Add the dill, shallot and white wine. Add the fish. Cover and steam gently over a low heat until cooked. Keep warm in the oven.

❸ Strain the fish juices through a fine sieve and pour into a small saucepan. Boil the liquid down almost completely. Add the tomato sauce and bring to the boil. Stir in the tomato strips and tarragon. Season with herb salt and pepper. Add the pieces of butter, one at a time.

❹ Cook the peas in salted water and drain.

❺ Pour the tomato sauce onto four warmed plates and arrange the fish and peas on top.

**Serves 4. About 320 kcal per serving**

# Sea bass in tomato butter

Sea bass is also known in Provence as "loup de mer" or "sea-wolf" because of its threatening appearance. It has few bones and the delicate flesh is delicious.

200 g/7 oz mangetouts
  (snow peas)

200 g/7 oz pumpkin

50 g/2 oz dried tomatoes

600 g/1¼ lb sea bass fillets

salt

pepper

1 clove garlic

1 shallot

2 tablespoons olive oil

1 sprig rosemary

50 ml vegetable stock (broth)

1 teaspoon chopped fresh savory

For the tomato butter:

500 g/18 oz over-ripe tomatoes

1 clove garlic

100 ml/3½ fl oz (½ cup) vegetable
  stock (broth)

some balsamic vinegar

25 g/1 oz (2 tablespoons) chilled
  butter pieces

2 tablespoons whipped cream

herb salt

freshly ground pepper

1 small bunch basil, cut into
  strips

❶ To make the tomato butter: remove the stalks and cut in half. Peel the clove of garlic and crush. Purée the tomatoes and garlic with the vegetable stock (broth) in the liquidizer.

❷ Put the puréed tomatoes in a saucepan, bring to the boil and then strain through a clean cloth. Reduce the liquid to 100 ml/3½ oz (scant ½ cup).

❸ Cut the mangetouts (snow peas) into diamond shapes and cook in the steam until ready. Peel the pumpkin and cut into small cubes. Dice the dried tomatoes.

❹ Season the sea bass fillets with salt and pepper. Peel the clove of garlic and shallot and chop both finely. Heat the olive oil in a pan, add the onion, garlic and rosemary and fry briefly. Add the fish fillets and fry, turning the fish now and again. Just before they are ready, remove them from the pan and put to one side.

❺ Fry the pumpkin and dried tomatoes in the remaining fat. Add the vegetable stock (broth), mangetouts (snow peas) and season with salt, pepper and savory. Return the fish fillets to the pan and finish cook until done.

❻ Add a little balsamic vinegar to the reduced tomato stock (broth). Add pieces of cold butter to the tomato stock (broth), stirring constantly. Fold in the whipped cream. Season the tomato butter with salt and butter. Add the basil. Pour the tomato butter onto four warmed plates. Arrange the vegetables and fish fillets.

**Serves 4. About 400 kcal per serving**

# Cod fillets on a bed of tomato sauce with saffron spaghettini

Saffron consists of the dried stigmas of the crocus flower which is a plant native to the Mediterranean regions. It is a very fragrant spice which plays an important part in Mediterranean cuisine. It is ideal for dishes for special occasions. A little more time must be allowed to prepare it.

**1** Blanch the spinach leaves, squeeze dry and season with salt and pepper. Rinse the cod fillets, pat them dry and cut in half lengthways. Season with salt and pepper and put the spinach on top. Carefully roll the fish fillets and put into small timbale moulds or cups.

**2** Peel the tomatoes, cut into quarters and remove the seeds. Finely chop the tomato quarters. Heat the olive oil in a pan, add the chopped tomatoes and fry. Now add 60 ml/3 fl oz (6 tablespoons) water, the tomato purée and bay leaf. Stir in the powdered vegetable stock (broth) and herbs. Bring to the boil and simmer for 10 minutes. Remove from the heat. Season with salt and pepper. Remove the bay leaf.

**3** Bring a large saucepan of salted water to the boil and cook the spaghettini following the instructions on the packet. Drain and keep in a warm place.

**4** Cook the cod fillet over the hot steam. Add knobs of butter and saffron to the spaghettini and stir. Season with salt and pepper.

**5** Pour the tomato sauce onto four warmed plates, arrange the fish fillets on top and garnish with parsley. Serve with the saffron-flavoured spaghettini.

**Serves 4. About 683 kcal per serving**

300 g/10 oz leaf spinach

salt

freshly ground pepper

600 g/1¼ lb cod fillets

600 g/1¼ lb ripe tomatoes

1 tablespoon olive oil

10 g/2 teaspoons tomato purée

1 bay leaf

½ packet Italian herbs (frozen)

1 teaspoon powdered vegetable stock (broth)

500 g/18 oz spaghettini

15 g/½ oz (1 tablespoon) butter

12 filaments saffron

2 tablespoons chopped parsley

# Tomatoes stuffed with cheese and salmon

These sophisticated stuffed tomatoes, filled with onions, mushrooms, salmon fillet and Limburger cheese, are delicious and filling. Served with fried rocket, it makes an interesting main course.

8 beef tomatoes

butter for the mould

1 small red onion

100 g/3½ oz mushrooms

300 g/11 oz salmon fillet

1 bunch chives

300 g/10 oz Limburger cheese

salt

pepper

2 bunch rocket

3 tablespoons oil

❶ Cut the tops off the tomatoes and carefully hollow out with a teaspoon.

❷ Pre-heat the oven to 180°C (350°F), Gas mark 4. Butter a gratin dish generously.

❸ Peel the onions and clean the mushrooms. Cut both into thin slices. Remove the skin from the salmon with a sharp knife and cut into fine strips. Chop up the chives and dice the cheese finely. Stir all the ingredients together. Season with salt and pepper.

❹ Put the hollowed out tomatoes next to each other in the gratin dish and fill with the salmon and cheese mixture. Bake in the oven for about 20 minutes.

❺ Fry the rocket briefly in hot oil, season with salt and pepper. Serve the fried rocket with the stuffed tomatoes.

**Serves 4. About 466 kcal per serving**

# Shrimps with radicchio and tomatoes

A tasty shrimp recipe, cooked with tomatoes and radicchio which make a mouth-watering sauce. It is delicious eaten with unsalted Italian bread.

2 medium tomatoes

2 small chicory bulbs

4 tablespoons garlic-infused oil

24 large prawns (shrimps), peeled and without heads

salt

white pepper

lemon juice

❶ Quarter the tomatoes, remove the seeds and chop up. Cut the radicchio into fine strips.

❷ Heat the oil in a large pan and briefly fry the shrimps all over. Add the radicchio and tomatoes, stir and cover. Cook over a low flame for about 8 minutes, stirring now and again. Season with salt, pepper and lemon juice.

**Serves 4. About 220 kcal per serving**

# Mussels with wine and tomato sauce

The common mussel is an edible mollusc found and farmed all over in the world. It lives in the sea where it clings to posts and stones. For safety, fresh ones should only be eaten when there is an "r" in the month, that is from September to April.

3 cloves garlic

5 spring onions (scallions)

1 leek

¼ celeriac root

1 carrot

5 tablespoons vegetable oil

1 sprig rosemary

½ teaspoon chopped thyme

1 large can tomatoes
   (800 g/1¾ lb)

2 kg/4½ lb mussels

500 ml/17 fl oz (2¼ cups) dry
   white wine

salt

pepper

cayenne pepper

❶ Peel the garlic and cut into thin slices. Peel the spring onions (scallions) and cut into thin strips. Cut the leeks into thin strips. Peel the celeriac and carrot. Cut the celeriac into small cubes and slice the carrots.

❷ Heat the oil in a very large frying pan or saucepan. Add the prepared vegetables and fry briefly. Stir in the herbs and tomatoes with their juice. Simmer gently for about 15 minutes.

❸ Wash the mussels carefully under the tap, using a brush. Throw away any mussels that are already open.

❹ Add the wine to the tomato sauce and bring to the boil. Remove the rosemary and season the sauce with salt, pepper and cayenne pepper.

❺ Add the mussels to the tomato sauce. Cover and cook over a high heat until ready. Shake the saucepan vigorously now and again. After about 10 minutes, serve the mussels and sauce on four warmed plates. Throw away any mussels that have remained closed during cooking.

**Serves 4. About 326 kcal per serving**

# Spiced redfish parcels with tomatoes and spinach

400 g/14 oz medium tomatoes

4 rusks (zwieback crackers)

120 g/5 oz (⅝ oz) herb butter

4 redfish fillets (150 g/5 oz each)

salt

white pepper

ground allspice

600 g/1¼ lb leaf spinach, frozen

The redfish is wrapped in aluminium foil and baked in the oven so that it cooks in its own juices. This delicious fish is served with leaf-spinach and tomatoes. The spinach can be replaced with Swiss chard.

❶ Peel and cut the tomatoes into quarters and remove the seeds. Finely chop the tomato pieces. Put the rusks (zwieback crackers) in the liquidizer and turn them into crumbs. Stir half the herb butter into the crumbs.

❷ Pre-heat the oven to 200°C (400°F), Gas mark 6. Prepare four large pieces of aluminium foil.

❸ Rinse the redfish fillets and pat dry with kitchen paper. Season the fillets on one side with salt and pepper. Put each fillet with its seasoned side down on a piece of aluminium foil with its shiny side facing upwards.

❹ Sprinkle the redfish fillets with ground allspice and coat with the herb butter and rusk (zwieback cracker) mixture. Wrap up each fillet loosely so that the fillets have plenty of room in the foil. Bake the fish parcels in the oven for 20–30 minutes.

❺ In the meantime, cook the spinach following the instructions on the packet. As soon as the spinach is defrosted, add the chopped tomatoes and herb butter. Cook the tomato and spinach until ready and season with salt and pepper. Serve the vegetables with the redfish.

**Serves 4. About 489 kcal per serving**

# Prawns (shrimps) with tomato sauce

This delicious dish is very easy and quick to make: the prawns (shrimps) are prepared in an instant!

❶ Peel the tomatoes, cut into quarters and remove the seeds. Cut the tomato pieces into small cubes. Heat the olive oil in a pan, add the diced tomatoes and cook until the mixture thickens, stirring all the time. Season with herbs, salt, sugar and pepper. Put the sauce in a warm place.

❷ Stick the prawns (shrimps) on four wooden skewers. Heat the clarified butter in a large pan and fry the skewers on both sides for about 5 minutes over medium heat.

❸ Pour the tomato sauce on the plates and arrange the prawns (shrimps) on top. Sprinkle with salt and pepper.

**Serves 4. About 364 kcal per serving**

**8 ripe beef tomatoes**

**3 tablespoons olive oil**

**1 teaspoon dried Italian herbs**

**salt**

**1 pinch sugar**

**lemon pepper**

**24 large prawns (shrimps), without head and peeled**

**60 g/2 oz (4 tablespoons) clarified butter**

# Haddock with herbs and tomatoes

This is a delicious way of serving haddock fillet, baked on a bed of tomato slices with a cheese and cream sauce.

❶ Rinse the haddock and pat dry with kitchen paper. Sprinkle with lemon juice. Cut the tomatoes into slices.

❷ Pre-heat the oven to 200°C (400°F), Gas mark 6. Butter a gratin dish.

❸ Peel the shallots and cloves of garlic and chop finely. Chop the parsley. Put the butter (which should be at room temperature) in a bowl, add the herbs, shallots, garlic, breadcrumbs and half the grated Pecorino and work into a paste. Season with salt and pepper.

❹ Put the crème fraîche and cream in a bowl and stir until smooth. Add the rest of the Pecorino and stir again. Season with salt and pepper. Arrange the tomato slices in the gratin dish and pour the cheese and cream mixture over them. Put the haddock fillets on top. Sprinkle the fillets with a little salt and coat them with the herb mixture.

❺ Bake the haddock in the oven for 20–30 minutes.

**Serves 4. About 604 kcal per serving**

**800 g/1¾ lb haddock fillets**

**juice of 1 lemon**

**500 g/18 oz beef tomatoes**

**butter for the mould**

**2 shallots**

**1 clove garlic**

**1 bunch smooth parsley**

**3 tablespoons butter**

**1 teaspoon chopped thyme**

**1 teaspoon chopped marjoram**

**60 g/2 oz (1 cup) breadcrumbs**

**80 g/3 oz grated Pecorino**

**salt**

**pepper**

**100 g/3½ oz crème fraîche**

**150 ml/5 fl oz (⅝ cup) cream**

# Cod steaks with tomato and Ajvar purée

A combination of hot and cold. The fish is served hot and accompanied by a cold, tasty sauce, made from tomatoes and Ajvar, the ready-made paprika purée.

**4 cod steaks**

**1 teaspoon lime juice**

**250 g/9 oz plum tomatoes**

**50 g/2 oz Ajvar**

**1 teaspoon soya sauce**

**1 tablespoon tomato purée**

**sambal oelek**

**1 pinch sugar**

**salt**

**pepper**

**2 tablespoons butter**

❶ Rinse the cod, pat dry with kitchen paper and put on a plate. Sprinkle the fish with lime juice, cover with foil and stand in the refrigerator for about 20 minutes.

❷ Peel the tomatoes, cut into quarters and remove the seeds. Chop up the tomato pieces and put in the liquidizer together with the ready-made paprika purée, soya sauce and tomato purée. Blend at the highest speed. Season the puréed tomato mixture to taste with the Indonesian spice sambal oelek, sugar, salt, and pepper. Put in a cold place.

❸ Heat the butter in a large pan and add the cod steaks. Cover and cook the fish until ready, turning once. Just before the end, remove the lid and cook for about another 2 minutes.

❹ Season the cod steaks with salt and pepper and serve with the cold tomato sauce.

**Serves 4. About 193 kcal per serving**

# Beef steak with tomato and Cognac sauce

This dish owes its piquant taste to the addition of Worcestershire sauce and cognac. As soon as the cognac is flambéed, the alcohol disappears but the aroma comes to the fore.

**❶** Peel the shallots and cut into very thin slices. Wash the chives and chop finely. Pour hot water over the tomatoes. Peel, remove the stalks and chop coarsely.

**❷** Heat the olive oil and butter in a pan, season the steaks with salt and pepper and fry on both sides over a high heat but do not overcook the meat. Remove from the pan and keep in a warm place.

**❸** Take the pan from the heat, pour away the excess fat, add the cognac, set light to it and return to the heat until the flames have died down. Soften the shallots in the pan. Add the tomatoes, Worcestershire sauce, beef stock (broth), salt and pepper. Stir and bring to the boil.

**❹** Return the steaks to the frying pan and finish cooking. Arrange the steaks on a plate, reduce the sauce a little, add the chives and pour the sauce over the steaks.

**Serves 4. About 390 kcal per serving**

2 shallots

½ bunch chives

4 large tomatoes

1 tablespoon olive oil

15 g/½ oz (1 tablespoon) butter

8 beef steaks (about 750 g/1¾ lb)

salt

freshly ground pepper

3 tablespoons Cognac

1 tablespoon Worcestershire sauce

250 ml/8 fl oz (1 cup) beef stock (broth)

# Pork fillet (tenderloin) with tomatoes

This spicy meat dish can be served with pasta cooked *al dente*, boiled rice or a creamy risotto. If you are in hurry, it can simply be served with freshly baked white or wholemeal (whole wheat) bread. This recipe is also delicious made with chicken breasts.

❶ Wash the pork fillet (tenderloin), pat it dry and cut into strips or slices of similar size. Season generously with marjoram, lemon zest, caraway, salt and pepper.

❷ Peel the garlic cloves, onions and spring onions (scallions). Chop the garlic finely and cut the onions and spring onions (scallions) into fine strips. Peel the tomatoes, cut into quarters and remove the seeds. Cut the tomato pieces into small cubes.

❸ Heat the olive oil in a pan, add the garlic and fry. Add the pork and fry while turning the meat constantly. Remove the meat and garlic mixture from the pan and keep in a warm place.

❹ Now add the onions and spring onions (scallions) to the cooking fat and fry until transparent. Add the tomatoes and cook briefly. Season the tomato mixture with salt, pepper, basil and oregano.

❺ Arrange the pork fillet (tenderloin) on four plates and garnish with the vegetables.

**Serves 4. About 354 kcal per serving**

800 g/1¾ lb pork fillet
   (tenderloin)

2 teaspoons chopped marjoram

1 teaspoon grated lemon peel

½ teaspoon ground caraway

salt

freshly ground pepper

4 cloves garlic

2 onions

8 spring onions (scallions)

8 tomatoes, chopped

2 tablespoons olive oil

4 tablespoons chopped basil

1 tablespoon chopped oregano

# Meatballs with lime and tomato sauce

Like hamburgers, meat balls are made from seasoned minced (ground) meat, fried in a pan. This version is made of beef and pork, served with tomato sauce flavoured with lime juice.

❶ Soak the bread in the milk. Peel the onions and chop finely. Chop up the sage. Peel the tomatoes, cut into quarters and remove the seeds. Cut the tomato pieces into small cubes.

❷ Heat the butter in a pan and fry the chopped onion. Squeeze the bread to remove as much milk as possible, tear into small pieces and fry briefly in the pan. Transfer the onion and bread mixture to a bowl.

❸ Put the minced (ground) pork and beef, egg, flour and sage in the bowl with the bread and onion mixture. Knead well. Season with salt and pepper and make into small meat balls.

❹ Heat the oil in a large pan and fry the meat balls all over until brown. Put the meat balls in a bowl and pour the port over them.

❺ Put the diced tomatoes in the liquidizer and purée at the highest speed. Season with salt, tabasco, olive oil and lime juice. Serve the tomato sauce cold with the meat balls.

**Serves 4. About 601 kcal per serving**

2 rolls

250 ml/8 fl oz (1 cup) milk, lukewarm

1 onion

6 sage leaves

800 g/1¾ lb medium tomatoes

1 tablespoon butter

250 g/9 oz minced (ground) beef

250 g/9 oz minced (ground) pork

1 egg

1 tablespoon flour

salt

pepper

oil for the roast

4 tablespoons port wine

1–2 dashes Tabasco

4 tablespoons olive oil

1 tablespoon lime juice

# Chicken livers
# in tomato sauce

600 g/1¼ lb chicken livers

3 shallots

2 carrots

500 g/18 oz tomatoes

½ bunch thyme

4 tablespoons oil

salt

pepper

1 tablespoon ketchup

A "must" for those who enjoy liver: chicken livers served in a delicious tomato sauce flavoured with thyme. Wild rice makes an excellent accompaniment.

❶ Rinse the chicken livers and pat dry with kitchen paper. Peel the shallots and carrots and slice both finely. Peel the tomatoes, cut into quarters and remove the seeds. Cut the tomatoes into strips. Chop the thyme.

❷ Heat 2 tablespoons oil in a pan, add the livers and fry. Season with salt and pepper. Put to one side.

❸ Heat the remaining oil in a pan. Add the shallot rings and sliced carrots. Add the ketchup and stir well. Cook briefly. Add the tomatoes and spices and simmer for about 10 minutes.

❹ Heat up the chicken livers briefly and serve with the tomato sauce. Season again with salt and pepper just before serving.

**Serves 4. About 341 kcal per serving**

# Pork chops on a bed of tomatoes and apple

Pork has a special affinity with apples. In this dish, the delicious aroma of tomatoes and apples is enhanced by the addition of sugar, cloves and grated zest of orange. Serve with mashed potato.

1 can chopped tomatoes
(400 g/14 oz)

200 ml apple juice

50 ml/3 fl oz (6 tablespoons)
raspberry vinegar

1 teaspoon sugar

2 cloves

1 tablespoon grated orange zest

3 small russet apples

4 pork chops (150 g/5 oz each)

❶ Pre-heat the oven to 200°C (400°F), Gas mark 6. Drain the chopped tomatoes and put in a bowl. Add the apple juice, vinegar, sugar, cloves and orange zest and stir well. Peel the apples, cut into quarters and remove the cores. Cut the apple quarters into slices and add to the bowl with the other ingredients. Stir well.

❷ Fill a casserole with half the tomato and apple mixture. Arrange the chops next to each other on top. Cover with the rest of the tomato and apple mixture. Cover and put in the oven.

❸ After 20 minutes, remove the lid and continue cooking in the oven for a further 10 minutes.

**Serves 4. About 304 kcal per serving**

# Veal escalope with tomato and olive purée

In Italy, this dish is called Scaloppina alla Pizzaiola. But it is pizza-like only to the extent that the veal escalope is the equivalent of the pizza base with the tomato purée and melted mozzarella on top.

1 pack mozzarella (200 g/7 oz)

1 large can tomatoes
(800 g/1¾ lb)

16 black olives, stoned (pitted)

1 clove garlic

salt

sugar

pepper

4 escalopes

6 tablespoons olive oil

½ teaspoon chopped oregano

❶ Drain the tomatoes and mozzarella. Cut the cheese into four slices. Put the tomatoes in the liquidizer and purée at the highest speed. Chop the olives and add to the tomato purée with the pressed garlic. Add a little sugar and season generously with salt and pepper.

❷ Beat the escalopes lightly and sprinkle with a little salt. Heat the oil in a very large pan and add the escalopes. Cover them completely with tomato purée and sprinkle with oregano.

❸ As soon as the escalopes are cooked, cover each with a slice of mozzarella. Cover the pan. The escalopes are ready to be served as soon as the mozzarella begins to melt.

**Serves 4. About 556 kcal per serving**

# Sauces, juices and drinks

Undisputed tomato classics include Traditional tomato sauce for pasta (page 126), Tomato ketchup (page 131), Tomato juice (page 134,) and the cocktail known as a Bloody Mary (page 136). Tomatoes also play a vital part in other delicious preparations such as Pear and tomato chutney sauce (page 133), a relish served cold with meat or bread, and Tomato and avocado salsa (page 130), a spicy dip that is irresistible with tortilla chips.

# Traditional tomato sauce for pasta

800 g/1¾ lb beef tomatoes

2 shallots

1 clove garlic

2 tablespoons olive oil

salt

pepper

1 pinch sugar

1 tablespoon balsamic vinegar

Spaghetti with tomato sauce has become a classic which is always popular with everyone, whether as a first or main course. It is a good idea to prepare large amounts of the sauce in advance and freeze in individual portions. This makes it possible to conjure up a delicious meal in no time at all. The sauce is simply defrosted, and reheated while the pasta is cooked.

❶ Peel the tomatoes, cut into quarters and remove the seeds. Chop the tomatoes into small cubes. Peel the shallots and clove of garlic and chop finely.

❷ Heat the oil in a pan. Add the shallots and garlic and fry them. Then add the diced tomatoes and season with salt, pepper, sugar and vinegar. Bring to the boil and simmer for about 45 minutes over a low heat with the lid on. If the sauce becomes too thick, add a little water.

❸ Continue simmering the sauce for another 5 minutes. Season again to taste. Serve hot.

**Serves 4. About 87 kcal per serving**

# Tomato sauce for fish, meat and vegetables

1 onion, finely chopped

2 cloves garlic

1 kg/2¼ lb over-ripe tomatoes

1 teaspoon olive oil

2 tablespoons tomato purée

some vegetable stock (broth)

1 tablespoon fresh chopped herbs, for instance, basil, oregano, parsley

herb salt

freshly ground pepper

1 teaspoon honey

1 tablespoon balsamic vinegar

This universal tomato sauce will lift any dish. Whenever meat, fish or vegetables taste too bland or dry on their own, this simple home-made sauce will enhance the dish.

❶ Peel the onions and cloves of garlic and chop finely. Peel and cut the tomatoes into quarters and remove the seeds. Chop the tomato quarters into small cubes.

❷ Heat the olive oil in a saucepan, add the onions and garlic and fry until transparent. Stir in the tomato purée and vegetable stock (broth). Cook briefly. Add the diced tomatoes, stir and simmer without a lid over a low heat for about 30 minutes.

❸ Add the herbs and season with herb salt, pepper, honey and vinegar. Purée the sauce if preferred.

**Serves 4. About 90 kcal per serving**

# Tomato and honey sauce

This sweet, spicy sauce can be used to accompany a wide variety of dishes. It is delicious served hot with lamb cutlets, braised broccoli or potato cakes. It is also excellent cold with roast beef.

1 small onion

1 clove garlic

8 medium tomatoes

3 tablespoons basil-infused oil

2 tablespoons forest honey

1 tablespoon balsamic vinegar

salt

pepper

❶ Peel the onion and garlic clove. Chop both finely. Peel the tomatoes, cut into quarters and remove the seeds. Cut the tomato quarters into small cubes.

❷ Heat the oil in a pan. Add the onion with the garlic and fry. Add the diced tomatoes, honey, vinegar, salt and pepper and stir well. Cook the sauce until it thickens, stirring constantly.

❸ Season the tomato and honey sauce with salt and pepper according to taste. Serve hot or cold.

**Serves 4. About 126 kcal per serving**

# Tomato and haricot (white) bean sauce

The tomatoes and haricot (white) beans are cooked with bacon, onions, herbs and parsley to make a nourishing, tasty sauce. It is delicious served with pasta, gnocchi and fried meat.

600 g/1¼ lb white beans from the glass

800 g/1¾ lb beef tomatoes

3 shallots

1 clove garlic

150 g/5 oz streaky bacon

½ bunch smooth parsley

2 tablespoons oil

salt

pepper

❶ Drain the haricot (white) beans. Peel the tomatoes, cut into quarters and remove the seeds. Cut the tomato quarters into small cubes. Peel the shallots and clove of garlic and chop. Cut the breakfast bacon into small dice. Chop the parsley.

❷ Heat the oil in a pan and sweat the bacon. Add the shallots and garlic. Fry until transparent. Add the haricot (white) beans and diced tomatoes and cook to thicken the sauce for about 15 minutes, stirring constantly. Stir in the parsley and season with salt and pepper.

❸ Serve the tomato and haricot (white) bean sauce hot.

**Serves 4. About 442 kcal per serving**

# Tomato and onion sauce

A spicy sauce made from red onions and tomatoes, flavoured with cider vinegar and honey. It is delicious served with roast pork and beef, fish and potatoes boiled in their skins.

**1** Peel the onions and cloves of garlic. Dice the onions. Peel the tomatoes, cut into quarters and remove the seeds. Dice the tomato quarters finely.

**2** Heat the oil in a pan and braise the onions lightly. Add the tomatoes and simmer until the sauce begins to thicken, stirring constantly. Season with salt, pepper, vinegar and honey.

**3** Shortly before the sauce is ready, add the pressed garlic. Season again according to taste. Serve the tomato and onion sauce hot.

**Serves 4. About 179 kcal per serving**

5 red onions

1 clove garlic

800 g/1¾ lb beef tomatoes

5 tablespoons olive oil

salt

black pepper from the mill

1 tablespoon apple vinegar

1 tablespoon honey

# Tomato and avocado salsa

400 g/14 oz plum tomatoes

2 shallots

1 clove garlic

½ bunch smooth parsley

1 avocado

salt

¼ teaspoon chilli powder

juice of 1 lime

2 tablespoons crème fraîche

This salsa dip is made from tomatoes and avocado is a spicy dip for Mexican tortilla chips. It is also a tasty spread which is delicious on bread.

❶ Peel the tomatoes, cut into quarters and remove the seeds. Cut the tomato quarters into very small cubes. Peel the shallots and the garlic clove; chop finely. Coarsely chop the parsley. Cut the avocados in half lengthways, remove the stone (pit) and scoop out the flesh with a spoon; cut the avocado into small cubes.

❷ Mix all these ingredients together and season with chilli powder and lime juice. Stir the crème fraîche until smooth and add to salsa.

**Serves 4. About 131 kcal per serving**

# Tomato sauce for grilled dishes

2 cans tomatoes
  (400 g/14 oz each)

70 g/3 oz red onions

4 pickled gherkins

5 tablespoons sunflower oil

2 teaspoons sugar

salt

pepper

This tomato sauce is ideal for barbecues as well as for everyday fried food. The ingredients can be varied to taste. For a spicier sauce, add Tabasco or cayenne pepper, while for a milder, creamier one, add a tablespoon of crème fraîche.

❶ Drain the tomatoes and cut into thin slices. Peel the onions and chop finely. Dice the pickled gherkins finely.

❷ Heat the oil in a pan and braise the onions lightly. Add the tomatoes and gherkins. Season with sugar, salt and pepper. Cook the sauce until it begins to thicken, stirring constantly. Season again after cooking and leave to cool down. Pour into screw-top jars and store in the refrigerator. The sauce should not be kept long.

**6 servings. About 103 kcal per serving**

# Tomato ketchup

Tomato ketchup has its place in every refrigerator and is particularly popular with children. Various kinds of ketchup can be bought but none tastes as delicious as that which you make yourself!

❶ Peel the tomatoes, cut into quarters and remove the seeds. Cut the tomato quarters into small cubes and put in a pan. Add 5 tablespoons of water and bring to the boil. Season with vinegar, sugar, honey, ground cinnamon, nutmeg, salt and pepper.

❷ Simmer for about 1 hour, stirring now and again, until the sauce has thickened. Strain the sauce through a sieve and cook for another 10 minutes. Season to taste.

❸ Allow the sauce to cool down and pour into screw-top jars. Store in a refrigerator. The ketchup should not be kept long.

**Serves 4. About 363 kcal per serving**

1 kg/2¼ lb ripe beef tomatoes

2 tablespoons raspberry vinegar

2 tablespoons sugar

1 tablespoon honey

1 pinch ground cinnamon

1 pinch nutmeg

salt

pepper

# Tomato stock

This is a stock (broth) prepared from cooked home-pressed tomato juice. It is an ideal base for all kinds of soups and can be used instead of vegetable, meat or fish stock (broth). The stock (broth) has not been seasoned, so this should be adjusted appropriately when preparing the dish in which it is used.

❶ Peel the tomatoes and cut into small pieces. Put the chopped tomatoes in a stainless steel sieve. Press the tomatoes to extract all the liquid, catching the juice in a bowl.

❷ Put the tomato juice in a small saucepan and simmer over a low heat without a lid until it begins to thicken a little.

**Serves 4. About 174 kcal per serving**

1 kg/2¼ lb over-ripe tomatoes

# Tomato chutney sauce with morello cherries and apples

A thick, tasty sauce made from tomatoes, shallots, apples, morello cherries and spices. It is delicious served cold with roast pork, beef or turkey. It is also excellent as a sauce with a meat fondue.

500 g/18 oz tomatoes

250 g/9 oz shallots

250 g/9 oz russet apples

250 ml/8 fl oz (1 cup) red wine vinegar

200 g/7 oz morello cherries, drained

1 teaspoon grain mustard

120 g/4 oz (generous ½ cup) brown sugar

salt

pepper

❶ Peel the tomatoes, cut into quarters and remove the seeds. Peel the shallots and cut each into four. Peel the apples, cut into quarters and remove the cores.

❷ Put all these ingredients in a saucepan, add the vinegar and bring to the boil. Add the morello cherries, mustard seeds, sugar, salt and pepper and cook until the mixture becomes thick, stirring often.

❸ Season the chutney sauce again according to taste and pour into preserving jars. Store in the refrigerator. Use within 1 week of opening.

**Serves 4. About 230 kcal per serving**

# Pear and tomato chutney sauce

Pears and tomatoes make an excellent sweet-and-sour chutney sauce. It is a particularly good relish with savoury puff pastry rolls such as spring rolls, or with deep-fried vegetables.

❶ Drain the pears and dice them. Cut the tomatoes into quarters, remove the seeds and cut into thin strips. Sprinkle a little salt on the tomato strips. Peel the onions and cut into rings.

❷ Put the diced pears, tomato strips and onion rings in a saucepan, add vinegar and bring to the boil. Season with powdered mustard, pepper, sugar, salt and cinnamon sticks. Cook the mixture until thick, stirring repeatedly.

❸ Remove the cinnamon sticks after cooking and pour the chutney into preserving jars. Store in a refrigerator. Use within 1 week of opening.

**Serves 4. About 320 kcal per serving**

1 can pears (400 g/14 oz)

300 g/10 oz beef tomatoes

3 small red onions

250 ml/8 fl oz (1 cup) apple vinegar

1 teaspoon mustard powder

½ teaspoon white pepper

200 g/7 oz brown sugar

salt

1 cinnamon stick

# Tomato vinaigrette

Tomato vinaigrette is a delicate salad dressing made from thin strips of tomatoes, shallots and garlic, in vinegar and oil. It is delicious with all leaf salads such as lettuce, radicchio or curly endive.

❶ Cut the tomatoes in half, remove the seeds, cut into very fine strips and cut these in half again. Peel the shallots and cloves of garlic; chop finely.

❷ Whisk the tarragon vinegar, mustard, sugar, salt and pepper together in a bowl. Slowly add the oil and stir it in. Add the tomatoes and stir well. Season again to taste.

**Serves 4. About 573 kcal per serving**

4 Cherry-medium tomatoes

1 shallot

2 cloves garlic

125 ml/4 fl oz (1 cup) tarragon vinegar

½ teaspoon medium mustard

1 pinch sugar

salt

white pepper

250 ml/8 fl oz (1 cup) vegetable oil

# Tomato juice

Every sip of fresh home-made tomato juice is pure pleasure! If a liquidizer is not available, the tomatoes can be chopped as finely as possible and pressed through a fine sieve with a wooden spoon.

2 kg/4½ lb ripe beef tomatoes

1 teaspoon Italian herbs

2 tablespoons honey

2 pinches cardamom

salt

pepper

❶ Peel the tomatoes, remove the seeds and cut into small pieces. Put the chopped tomatoes in a liquidizer, add 2 tablespoons of water and purée at the highest speed until the mixture has turned into juice.

❷ Season the tomato juice to taste with herbs, honey, cardamom, salt and pepper. Pour into a jug, cover with clingfilm and cool in the refrigerator. Use within 24 hours.

**Serves 4. About 118 kcal per serving**

# Ice-cold lime and tomato tea

Green tea with vegetable and tomato juice, flavoured with lime juice and tabasco, makes a cool, refreshing, very tasty drink which is delicious not only on warm summer's days but any time of the year.

8 ice cubes

400 ml/14 fl oz (1¾ cups) cold green tea

200 ml/7 oz (⅞ cup) vegetable juice

200 ml/7 oz (⅞ cup) tomato juice

salt

pepper

Tabasco

2 tablespoons lime juice

❶ Wrap ice cubes in a tea towel and crush with a hammer. Put the crushed ice cubes in four tall drinking glasses.

❷ Mix the vegetable and tomato juice with the green tea; season with salt, pepper, tabasco and lime juice. Pour the the lime and tomato tea into the glasses and serve immediately.

**Serves 4. About 20 kcal per serving**

# Bloody Mary

12 ice cubes

600 ml/1 pint (2½ cups) tomato juice

80 ml/3 fl oz (⅜ cup) vodka

4 tablespoons lime juice

paprika

salt

white pepper

Tabasco

1 lime

A Bloody Mary is a vodka cocktail with highly-seasoned tomato juice. It is a delicious long drink when served ice-cold, and it is also an excellent aperitif, served just before the meal.

❶ Put the ice cubes in four tall drinking glasses.

❷ Stir the vodka and lime juice into the tomato juice; season with ground paprika, salt, pepper and a dash of tabasco.

❸ Pour the Bloody Mary over the ice cubes and garnish each glass with a slice of lime. Serve immediately.

**Serves 4. About 62 kcal per serving**

# Tomato sorbet with gin

55 g/2 oz (1/4 cup) sugar

750 g/1¾ lb tomatoes

100 ml/3½ fl oz (½ cup) gin

juice of 1 lime

sliced lime for the garnish

A sorbet is a semi-frozen dessert made from fruit pulp which was invented by the ancient Persians. It is often served with alcohol as a refreshment just before the main course of a large meal.

❶ Bring the sugar to the boil with 100 ml/3½ fl oz (scant ½ cup) water. Simmer gently until the sugar has completely dissolved, stirring constantly. Remove from the heat and leave to cool.

❷ Peel the tomatoes, cut into quarters and remove the seeds. Chop the tomato pieces finely and put in a saucepan. Simmer over a low heat for about 20 minutes, stirring occasionally.

❸ Purée the tomatoes with the sugar solution in a liquidizer or with a hand-mixer. Put this mixture in a freezer box and put in the freezer compartment. Stir from time to time with a whisk as it freezes.

❸ Divide the tomato sorbet into six portions and put them in cold glasses or glass bowls. Mix the gin and lime juice and sprinkle over the sorbet. Garnish with slices of lime and serve immediately.

**Serves 6. About 86 kcal per serving**

# Cooking glossary

# Glossary of technical and foreign language cooking terms

## baking, roasting

Cooking food in the oven in a heat-resistant dish, in a baking tin (pan) or on a baking (cookie) sheet. The food is cooked by the hot air of a conventional or a fan oven (in a fan oven the same cooking effect is achieved with a lower temperature; see the maker's manual). The temperature most commonly used is 180°C (350°F), Gas Mark 4, which is ideal for cakes, biscuits (cookies), tarts, flans, roasts, fish and poultry. For puff pastry, soufflés and gratins the temperature should be between 200°C (400°F), Gas mark 6 and 220°C (425°F), Gas mark 7. More delicate food such as fish, veal and some poultry may need a lower heat, from 150°C (300°F), Gas mark 2 to 160°C (325°F), Gas mark 3.

As a rule of thumb, the lower the temperature, the longer the cooking time.

## bain-marie

A container of hot water in which or over which food is gently cooked. It may be a rectangular pan in which pans are placed, but in the domestic kitchen it usually takes the form of a double boiler, a saucepan with a smaller pan fitting over it. It can be improvised satisfactorily by using a bowl over a saucepan containing about 2.5 cm/1 inch of hot water.

A bain-marie is used when it is essential not to overheat what is being cooked. It is used for processes such as melting chocolate, and for cooking sauces or puddings containing cream or eggs. For instance, to make a chocolate mousse, the egg whites are beaten stiff over a warm bain-marie. This makes a particularly airy, light yet firm mousse. A bain-marie is also indispensable for making a successful Hollandaise or Béarnaise sauce. The egg yolks are slowly heated while being stirred until they reach the correct consistency, so that they combine with the melted butter whisked into it little by little.

## barding

Covering very lean meat such as saddle of venison, pheasant or saddle of hare with slices of bacon, secured with kitchen string. This ensures that the meat remains juicy and does not dry out, while also adding a pleasant flavour to the meat.

## basting

Spooning liquid over food while it is being roasted. Normally the cooking juices are used, but butter, wine, stock (broth) or plain water can be used as well. This constant basting and 'looking after' the meat ensures that it remains juicy and does not dry out. The basting liquid acquires a very intense flavour.

## beurre manié

Kneaded butter, used to thicken casseroles

and sauces. Equal amounts of flour and butter are kneaded together and added as small knobs into boiling liquid while stirring constantly. This thickening agent has a delicious buttery taste and it is easy to handle because the butter and flour are mixed before being adding to the liquid, reducing the risk of lumps forming in the course of cooking.

## blanching

Cooking vegetables such as spinach, leeks and carrots briefly in fast-boiling water. It is important to refresh the vegetables by plunging them in ice-cold water immediately afterwards. This ensures that the vegetables remain crisp and retain their original colour. After blanching, the vegetables are heated in hot stock (broth) or butter before serving.

## blini

Pancake (crepe) made of a Russian batter using buckwheat flour, fried in a special small frying pan (skillet) about 15 cm (6 in) in diameter. Wheat flour is often added to the buckwheat flour so that it binds more easily. Blinis are usually served with caviar. They are also delicious with braised meat and game.

## boiling

Cooking in liquid that is boiling. The process is synonymous with the concept of cooking. The food is cooked in a large amount of water and the agitation of the liquid will prevent the ingredients sticking to each other. So long as the water is boiling, the temperature will be 100°C (212°F) for the whole of the cooking time.

## bouquet garni

A small bundle of various fresh herbs (usually parsley, thyme and bay leaves), tied together and cooked with the food. The bouquet garni is removed before serving.

## braising

This refers to a method of cooking which combines frying, simmering and steaming. First the food is seared in hot oil or fat on all sides. This seals the meat, forming a thin crust; this also forms roasting matter on the bottom of the pan which is very important for the colour and flavour of the sauce. Liquid is then added to the meat, the pan is sealed with a lid and the food is slowly braised in a preheated oven. The method is also good for vegetable and fish dishes. It is excellent for less tender, strongly flavoured cuts of meat such as oxtail, goulash, braising steak or stewing lamb.

## breadcrumbs

Dried white crumbs, made from stale bread without the crust. They are used in stuffing mixtures or to coat fish, poultry or other meats such as lamb chops.

## brunoise

Finely diced vegetables or potatoes.

## canapé

Small, bite-sized pieces of bread with various toppings such as smoked salmon, foie gras, caviar, smoked duck breast, ham and so on. They are served as an appetizer.

## carcass

The carcass of poultry used in the preparation of chicken stock (broth). Fish bones are used in a similar way to make fish stock (broth).

## carving

Cutting meat or poultry into slices or small pieces for serving. It is a good idea to carve on a carving board with a groove for the juices, using a special carving knife.

## casserole

A large heat-resistant cooking pot usually made of cast iron or earthenware, excellent for slow-cooked dishes, braises and stews such as oxtail and game ragout. Because of the casserole's large surface area and the lengthy cooking time, the meat is able to release its full flavour. Casseroles may be round or oval, the latter shape being ideally suited for long-shaped pieces of meat such as leg of lamb, rolled cuts of meat or a chicken.

## célestine

Fine strips of pancake (crepe) added to soup as a garnish.

## chiffonade

Finely cut strips of lettuce, often served with shrimp cocktail.

## chinois

Conical strainer or sieve used to strain sauces and soups.

## clarification

The removal of cloudy matter from soups, stock (broth) or jelly with lightly beaten egg white. The egg white attracts all the foreign particles which cause the cloudiness and they can then be easily removed. The operation is carried out as follows. A lightly beaten egg white is added to some lean minced (ground) beef and chopped vegetables and a few ice cubes are stirred in. The mixture is added to the stock (broth), which should also be well chilled. Heat up while stirring constantly. The egg white begins to thicken at 70°C (160°F) and in the process it attracts all the impurities in the stock (broth). The stock (broth) becomes clear while developing a very intense flavour, as a result of the beef and vegetables. Fish and vegetable stock (broth) can also be clarified in the same way; in these cases the meat is omitted.

## coating

The operation of pouring sauce over vegetables, meat or fish.
  It also describes the technique of covering slices of meat and fish with beaten egg and breadcrumbs before frying them in hot oil. This gives the food a crisp coating while keeping the inside moist and juicy.

## concassée

Blanched, peeled, quartered and de-seeded tomatoes, finely chopped. The term may also be applied to herbs.

## consommé

Simple soup made of meat or chicken stock (broth), sometimes garnished. When clarified, it is known as clear or "double" consommé. Cold consommé is often a jelly.

## cream soup, velouté soup

Cream soups are thickened with béchamel sauce. Velouté soups are thickened with an egg and cream mixture. The soup should not be brought back to the boil after the mixture has been added because the egg yolk would curdle.

## crepes

Thin pancakes made from a batter consisting of milk, flour and eggs. The pancakes are cooked slowly in a frying pan (skillet) until golden. They can be served as a dessert, plain with a sprinkling of sugar and lemon juice, or spread or filled with jam or chocolate. They can also be served as a savoury dish, stuffed with vegetable or other fillings.

## deep-frying

The process of cooking food by immersion in hot fat. When the food is cooked and crisp, it is removed from the fat or oil in its basket or with a skimming ladle and left to drain thoroughly on kitchen paper. Because hot oil or fat often spatters it is vital to be extremely careful and avoid the risk of fire. An electric chip pan with an adjustable thermostatically controlled temperature control is an excellent idea not only because it is safer but it also creates much less of a smell. Peeled potatoes cut into chips (sticks) or slices, shrimps and vegetables in batter are ideal for deep-frying, while deep-fried semolina dumplings are delicious served in soup. Deep-frying is also used for sweet dishes such as doughnuts and apple fritters.

## duxelles

Garnish or stuffing consisting of finely chopped mushrooms sweated with diced onions and herbs.

## forcemeat or stuffing

Finely chopped meat or fish used to stuff eggs, meat, pasta and so on. It can make a dish in its own right, as in the case of meat balls and quenelles, for example. It is also used as a basis for terrines and pâtés such as deer terrine or wild boar pâté.

## filleting

The operation of cutting off the undercut of beef sirloin or similar cuts of pork (tenderloin), veal or lamb; removing the breasts of poultry from the carcass; or cutting the flesh of fish in strip-like pieces from the backbone.

## flambé

Pouring spirits (such as brandy, rum or Grand Marnier) over food and setting light to it. The process is used with both savoury and sweet dishes, such as Crêpes Suzette. The spirits need to be warmed slightly first.

## fleurons

Small pieces of puff pastry baked into various shapes such as flowers, little ships or shrimps. They are served with fish dishes in a sauce or with chicken fricassée.

## flouring

The coating of pieces of fish or meat with flour before frying. This forms a tasty crust round the meat or fish which will be particularly juicy as a result.

## frying

Frying is the process of cooking food in hot fat. The best fats and oils for frying are therefore ones that can be heated to a high temperature such as sunflower oil, clarified butter or goose fat. When butter is used, a little oil is often added to raise the temperature it will reach without burning. Some cuts of meat such as beef steaks or pork cutlets may be fried in a non-stick griddle pan without any fat.

## gazpacho

Cold Spanish vegetable soup made with fresh tomatoes, cucumbers, garlic and fresh herbs. It is particularly delicious on a hot summer's day.

## glazing

Creating a glossy surface on vegetables, meat, fish or puddings. A suitable stock (broth), the cooking juices, a light caramel, jelly, hot jam or icing is poured over the food in question.

## gnocchi

Small dumplings, originally Italian, made from potato, semolina or bread flour, depending on the region, poached briefly in boiling water.

## gratiné

Baking dishes under a very high top heat until a brown crust has formed. The ideal topping is grated cheese, breadcrumbs or a mixture of the two.

## grilling (broiling)

Cooking with intense radiant heat, provided by gas, electricity or charcoal, the latter giving the food a particularly delicious flavour. The food is cooked on a grid without fat, and grilling (broiling) is therefore particularly good for people who are calorie conscious. Meat, fish, poultry and even vegetables can be cooked in this way.

## healthy eating

A well-balanced, varied diet based on wholesome, nutritious foods in the right proportion. Ingredients recommended include wholemeal (wholewheat) products, organic meat, fish and poultry and fresh fruit and vegetables.

## julienne

Peeled vegetables cut into thin sticks, the length and thickness of matchsticks. They are cooked in butter or blanched and used as a garnish for soup, fish, meat or poultry dishes.

## jus

The name given to cooking juices produced during roasting. It is also used to describe brown stock (broth) prepared from various kinds of meat.

## kaltschale

Literally "cold cup", this is a cold sweet soup made with fruit and wine. The fruit, for instance raspberries, melon and strawberries, is finely puréed with lemon juice and wine if so desired to which fresh herbs are added. It is important that it is served chilled.

## larding needle

Special needle for pulling lardons (strips of pork fat) through lean meat to keep it moist and make it more tender.

## marinade

A mixture based on vinegar, lemon juice, buttermilk or yoghurt, with onions and other vegetables, spices and herbs. Meat or fish is steeped in the mixture for several hours to make it tender and enhance its flavour. Marinades can also be used for dressing salads or for marinating meat that is already tender. Meat marinades give sauces a particularly delicious flavour because they have absorbed the various flavours from the herbs, vegetables and spices.

## marinating

Steeping meat or fish in a liquid containing salt, wine, vinegar, lemon juice or milk, and flavourings such as herbs and spices. Marinating has a tenderizing effect on the food and also improves the flavour because of the various ingredients added to the marinade. In addition, marinating also has a preserving effect on meat or fish so that it keeps longer. For instance, raw salmon may be marinated in salt, sugar, herbs and spices.

## minestrone

Classic Italian vegetable soup using a wide variety of vegetables, the selection depending on the region and the season. However, pasta and beans are essential ingredients.

## mirepoix

Finely diced vegetables, often with the addition of bacon and herbs, fried in butter and used as a basis for sauces.

## muffins

Round, flat rolls made with yeast dough and baked. In America, muffins are sweet rolls, using baking powder as a raising agent, made in special muffin pans. There are many varieties made, for instance with blueberries, raspberries, red currants or chocolate.

## pie

A sweet or savoury dish baked in a pastry shell with a pastry top. It is made in a pie tin (pan) with a slanting edge 5 cm (2 in) high. The lid of dough should have a small opening in the middle so that the steam can escape, preventing the pie crust from swelling up.

## ramekin or cocotte

A small, round oven-proof china or earthenware dish in which individual portions are cooked and served.

## reducing

Concentrating a liquid by boiling it so that

the volume is reduced by evaporation. It increases the flavour of what is left. Strongly reducing a sauce gives a particularly tasty result with a beautiful shine.

## refreshing

Dipping food, particularly vegetables, briefly in cold water after cooking to preserve the colour, mineral content and vitamins. The cooked vegetables or other items are then drained in a colander.

## roasting

See baking.

## roux

A mixture of butter and flour used to thicken sauces. The mixture is made by melting butter and stirring in flour. This is then diluted with milk or stock (broth) and cooked for at least 15 minutes while stirring constantly. For a dark roux, the flour is cooked until it turns brown before liquid is added. Because this reduces the thickening quality of the flour, the amount of flour should be increased.

## royale

A custard-like cooked egg garnish. Milk and eggs are stirred together, seasoned, poured into small buttered moulds and poached in a bain-marie at 70–80°C (160–180°F). They are then turned out and diced.

## salamander

Electric appliance used to caramelize or brown the top of certain dishes. It is comparable to a grill, which is normally used as a substitute.

## sauté

Cooking food in fat in a frying pan (skillet). Small, uniform pieces of meat, fish, chopped vegetables or sliced potatoes are cooked in a pan while being tossed to prevent them sticking. In this way all sides of the food are cooked.

## simmering

Cooking food in liquid over a low heat, just below boiling point. This method of cooking is often used for making soups and sauces since it makes the food tender and enables it to develop its full aroma.

## soufflé

Particularly light, aerated dish made with beaten egg white which may be sweet or savoury. A meal which finishes with a mouth-watering chocolate soufflé will always be remembered with great pleasure.

## soup bones

Meat bones, poultry carcass or fish bones used in making stock (broth). These are very important ingredients because they give an intense flavour to the stock (broth). Smooth beef and veal bones are ideal, but the marrow bone has the most flavour. It is important that the bones should be purchased from a reliable butcher and come from a guaranteed source so as to avoid any risk of BSE (mad cow disease).

## steaming

Cooking over boiling water so that the food is out of contact with the liquid and cooks in the steam. To achieve this, the food is cooked in a perforated container over lightly boiling water or stock (broth). This method of cooking ensures that vegetables keep their flavour particularly well. They remain crisp and full of taste. Fish too can be cooked in this way without any additional fat but simply with herbs and spices. Steaming is particularly good for the preparation of low-calorie dishes for people who must follow a low-fat diet for reasons of health. But it will also appeal to everyone who loves the pure, genuine flavour of food.

## stock (broth)

The flavoured liquid base of soups and sauces. Basic meat stocks (broths) for soups and sauces are made by simmering meat and bones of veal, beef, game, poultry or fish for several hours. As the liquid simmers gently, the constantly forming foam is periodically removed with a skimming ladle. When the stock (broth) has cooled down, the layer of fat can be removed so that the stock (broth) becomes light and clear. Vegetable stock (broth) is made in a similar way by boiling vegetables and herbs

## straining

Filtering solid matter from liquids or draining liquids from raw or cooked food. Soups, sauces and stock (broth) are poured or pressed through a fine sieve. In the case of a stock (broth) the sieve may be lined with a coarse cloth.

## string

Kitchen string is used to truss poultry or to tie a joint of meat so that it keeps its shape while being cooked.

## suprême

Breast of chicken or game. The name refers to the best part of the bird, which is always prepared with the greatest care.

## sweating

Frying the food lightly in a little fat in a pan over moderate heat, so that it softens but does not brown.

## tartlet

Small tart made from short crust or puff pastry with a sweet or savoury filling.

## tenderizing

Making tough meat tender by beating it. The meat is placed between two sheets of foil and beaten with a mallet or the bottom of a small pan until it has become thin. It is used for roulades, veal escalopes and so on.

## thickening

The addition of a substance to a sauce or soup to thicken it. There are several common methods. Flour may be added and stirred continuously until the liquid thickens. A variation is to mix butter and flour as a roux to which the liquid is slowly added, again stirring constantly. Alternatively egg yolk or cream can be stirred into the liquid to make an emulsion. On no account must it be allowed to boil or it will curdle. After the yolk has been stirred into the sauce or soup, it must not be cooked any more or it will curdle.

## timbale

Mould lined with pastry, blind-baked and filled with meat, fish or other ingredients in a sauce, baked in the oven or cooked in a bain-marie.

## trimming

The removal of connective tissue and fat from all kind of meats. The off-cuts are used in the preparation of stock (broth) and sauces. It is important to use a very sharp knife, held flat against the meat so as not to remove too much meat in the process.

## turning

Forming vegetables and potatoes into decorative shapes, such as balls, ovals or spirals. This is carried out using a small knife with a crescent-shaped blade.

## zest

The thin outer rind of oranges or lemons, used for its flavour and fragrance. It is cut from the pith in thin strips, using a zester.

# Herbs and spices

### agar

Thickening agent made from dried algae from Asia. It is used as a vegetable gelling agent, for instance, in the manufacturing of blancmange powder, jelly or processed cheese. Agar only dissolves in very hot liquid and has highly gelatinous properties. It is therefore important to follow the instructions very carefully. It is particularly useful in vegetarian cuisine where it is an alternative to gelatine, which is made from beef bones. Agar is often combined with other thickening agents such as carob bean flour because it is very indigestible. This makes it a much more effective thickening agent.

### allspice

These brown berries are grown in tropical countries, particularly Jamaica. The complex, multi-layered aroma of allspice is at its best when the fresh grains are crushed in a mortar. It is used to season lamb and beef ragouts, sausages, pies and gingerbread.

### aniseed

Aniseed is often associated with the delicious aroma of Christmas cakes and pastries. The seed can be used whole, crushed or ground. It is also used in savoury dishes, for instance in the seasoning and marinades of fish and preparation of fish stock (broth). It is the main flavour of alcoholic drinks such as pastis and ouzo.

### basil

Basil is undoubtedly the king of all fresh herbs used in the kitchen. It is an aromatic annual herb that plays an important part in a wide variety of dishes. It has a particular affinity with tomatoes and it is used in salads and many Mediterranean dishes.

### basil, Thai

Thai basil is an important herb in Thai cuisine, used in baked noodle dishes, sauces and curries. It is available in many shops specialising in eastern food. It is very delicate and should be used as fresh as possible.

### bay leaves

The leathery leaves of the bay tree have a spicy, bitter taste which becomes even stronger when dried. It is one of the ingredients of a bouquet garni. The fresh leaves are added to fish, when dried it is an important ingredient of many preserved dishes, such as braised meat marinated in vinegar and herbs, or pickled gherkins.

### borage

A herb with hairy leaves and wonderful blue flowers. It has a slightly bitter, tangy taste reminiscent of cucumber and is mainly used in drinks such as Pimms. It is also a good accompaniment to salads, soups, cabbage and meat dishes.

### burnet, salad

The leaves must be harvested before the plant flowers. Salad burnet is used in the same way as borage. It is only used fresh since it loses its aroma completely when dried.

## caraway

Caraway is the traditional spice used in rich, fatty dishes such as roast pork, sauerkraut, raw cabbage dishes and stews – not simply for its aromatic flavour but also because of its digestive properties. It is added to some cheeses. Whole or ground, it is also used in spiced bread and cakes. Many liqueurs contain caraway because of its digestive properties.

## cardamom

After saffron, cardamom is one of the most expensive spices in the world. Removed from the pod, the seeds are used ground. Just a pinch will be enough to add a delicious taste to rice dishes, cakes or gingerbread.

## chervil

The fine flavour of chervil will enhance any spring or summer dish. It can be used in salads, soups and fish dishes and it is also very decorative.

## chilli peppers

Red or green chilli peppers are hot and add a spicy, aromatic pungency to food. They are available fresh, dried, ground, pickled or in the form of a paste or essence (extract). When using fresh peppers, it is advisable to remove the seeds which are the hottest part. They are especially popular in Central and south-western America, the West Indies and

Asia, forming an integral part of many dishes originating in these regions.

## chives

This is one of the great traditional cooking herbs which is available throughout the year. Very versatile, chives are sold fresh in bunches and are delicious with fromage frais, bread and butter, scrambled eggs or fresh asparagus. The beautiful blue flowers of the chive plant are very decorative and also delicious, making a great addition with the leaves to any salad in the summer.

## cloves

The flower buds of the clove tree have an intensely spicy aroma with a bitter, woody taste. That is why it should be used sparingly. Cloves are used in marinades, red cabbage and braised dishes as well as in mulled wine and many Christmas cakes and buns.

## coriander (cilantro)

Coriander seeds have been used for a long time, mainly as a pickling spice and in Oriental dishes. Fresh green coriander leaves (cilantro) have become available in many countries much more recently. Finely chopped, this sweetish spicy herb adds an exotic aroma to many dishes, including guacamole. It should be used with discretion by those who are not used to the taste.

## cress

The small-leafed relative of the watercress is slightly less aromatic. It is usually sold as small plants in paper containers or as seeds to grow oneself, often with mustard as the mustard and cress used in elegant sandwiches. Cress is commonly used to garnish egg dishes and salads.

## cumin

This classic spice is common in eastern cuisine and is a fundamental ingredient of curry powder and curry pastes. It adds an interesting, exotic flavour to braised dishes such as lamb, kid or beef.

## curry powder

Curry powder may be made from as many as 30 spices, including among others turmeric, pepper, cumin, caraway, cloves, ginger and allspice. It is extremely versatile and in addition to its use in curries it can be used in small quantities to add flavour to many meat, fish and poultry dishes.

## dill

An annual sweetish aromatic herb, common in northern European cooking but seldom used in Mediterranean dishes. The feathery leaves are used fresh in fish dishes, sauces, with fromage frais, and in vegetable dishes. Cucumber pickles (dill pickles) make use of the leaves and the seeds.

## fennel

Fennel leaves have a slight flavour of aniseed and are commonly used with fish. The seeds are sometimes used to season bread. When added to fish dishes and fish stock (broth), the seeds are crushed first.

## fines herbes

Classic French combination of herbs, made from parsley, tarragon, chervil, chives, and perhaps thyme, rosemary and other herbs. Fines herbes may be used fresh, dried or frozen. The commonest use is in omelettes.

## galangal

A close relative of the ginger family which is much used in south-eastern cuisine. The roots can used fresh, dried, ground or dried.

## garam masala

The meaning of this Indian name is 'hot mixture', and it consists of up to 13 spices. It plays an important part in the cooking of India, where it is home-made, so that its composition varies from family to family. Garam masala is available commercially in supermarkets and in shops specialising in Asian food.

## garlic

Cooking without garlic is unimaginable to anyone who loves and enjoys the pleasures of the Mediterranean. Freshly chopped, it enhances salads and cold sauces, roasts, stews, braised and grilled (broiled) dishes, all benefit from the addition of garlic. Another popular use is in garlic bread.

## gelatine

Gelatine is a thickening agent made from beef bones. Leaf gelatine must be soaked thoroughly in plenty of cold water for five or ten minutes before using it. It is then squeezed well and diluted in warm water. A special technique is needed when using gelatine in cream-based dishes. A few spoonfuls of cream are stirred into the gelatine. This mixture is then stirred into the rest of the cream. In this way lumps will be avoided.

## ginger

The juicy roots of ginger have a sharp fruity aroma. Ginger adds an interesting, exotic touch to both savoury and sweet dishes. Because ginger freezes very well it can be kept for a long time without losing any of its flavour. A piece can be broken off whenever it is needed.

## lavender

The taste of lavender is bitter and spicy. It can be used as a seasoning for lamb-based dishes, meat and fish stews and salads. The flowers are particularly decorative.

## lovage

Lovage has a celery-like taste and both the stems and the leaves can be used in soup, salads and sauces. The finely chopped leaves are sometimes added to bread dumplings, and to the stuffing for breast of veal to which it adds a particularly delicate flavour.

## marjoram

Sweet marjoram is a popular herb with a distinctive aroma. It can be used either fresh and dried, but like almost all herbs it is best when it is fresh. Marjoram is delicious in potato soups and omelettes. Pot marjoram is

a hardier form with a stronger flavour, so it is advisable not to use too much.

## mint

Mint is delicious as mint tea and also in puddings such a mint ice cream, and in drinks. It is part of many soups, salads and meat dishes, and is often added to potatoes and peas. Mint sauce is served with lamb. Mint leaves are also often used as decoration.

## mugwort

This is a variety of wormwood. It grows in the wild and the sprigs should be collected just before the plants flower. They can also be dried for later use. Mugwort is popular with roast goose and game.

## mustard seeds

Mustard seeds are one of the most important ingredients in pickled vegetables such as gherkins, courgettes (zucchini), pumpkin, mixed pickles and pickled cocktail onions. They are often used too in braised beef, marinated in vinegar and herbs.

## nasturtiums

Nasturtium flowers are very decorative and the leaves are delicious, their sharp, peppery taste adding a spicy touch to any salad.

## nutmeg

Grated nutmeg is delicious in soups, stews, potato purée and cabbage. It is a also a traditional seasoning in Christmas cakes and confectionery. It tastes best when freshly grated.

## oregano

Also known as wild marjoram, oregano is much used in Italian cuisine. It is essential in many dishes such as pizzas, pasta with tomato sauce and aubergine (egg plant) dishes. In the case of pizzas it is best to use dried oregano because the fresh leaves become brown in the very strong heat of the hot oven, thus losing much of their flavour.

## parsley

The most popular of all herbs, two varieties are common, one with curly leaves and the other with smooth leaves. But it is not only the leaves that are used; the roots too are full of flavour and are delicious added to soups and sauces. Parsley has a deliciously fresh aroma and a strong taste. It is also extremely rich in vitamins and minerals, so it is an important herb for use in winter.

## pepper

Black pepper and white pepper have different tastes as well as looking different. Black pepper is obtained by harvesting the unripe fruit, while white pepper is the ripe fruit which is peeled before being dried. White pepper is milder, more delicate in taste and not as sharp as black.

## purslane

The green, fleshy leaves can be used raw in salads or used as a vegetable in its own right as in the Far East. The delicious leaves have a slightly salty flavour.

## rosemary

Rosemary has a particular affinity with lamb, which is often roasted with a few sprigs. It is particularly popular in France where it is used in many dishes such as soups, potatoes, vegetables, meat and fish dishes. Dried, chopped rosemary is one of the ingredients of *herbes de Provence*.

## saffron

This bright orange spice is the 'golden' condiment of good cuisine, providing an inimitable flavour and colour. It consists of the dried stigmas of the saffron crocus, and about 4,000 of these are needed for 25 g (1 oz), which accounts for its high cost. But only a small amount is needed; just a few filaments or a tiny pinch of ground saffron will be enough to add a very special taste to bouillabaisse, paella or risotto.

## sage

The sharp, slightly bitter taste of sage is ideal with roast goose or roast lamb. Often used in sausages, it is also one of the most important ingredients of the Italian classic 'Saltimbocca' (veal escalope with sage and Parma ham). The fresh leaves are delicious dipped in batter and fried.

## savory

Savory is a peppery herb used in many bean-based dishes and also in stews and casseroles. The stem is cooked in the stew while the young shoots are chopped up and added to the dish just before the end of the cooking time.

### star anise

This is the small star-shaped seed of the Chinese aniseed, native to China. The flavour is a little more bitter than aniseed itself. It can be used for baking and cooking and adds a delicious flavour to leg of lamb and dried apricots or in sweet and sour beef stew. It can also be used in puddings such as apple or quince compote.

### tamarind

The pods contains a very sour juice which is much used in Indian and Thai cooking. Dishes such as baked fish with tamarind sauce, cherry tomatoes and fresh ginger are quite delicious.

### tarragon

Tarragon has a delicate, spicy flavour. It can be used on its own as in tarragon vinegar or tarragon mustard, in Béarnaise as well as in a wide range of poultry and fish dishes. It is also excellent when combined with other herbs such as chervil, chives and parsley. The variety to be used is French tarragon. Russian tarragon grows easily from seed but has little flavour.

### thyme

Like rosemary, this sweetish spicy herb is particularly good with Mediterranean food. It is an essential part of a bouquet garni and one of the main ingredients of *herbes de Provence*. Thyme will add a special touch to any dish, whether meat, fish, poultry or vegetables.

### turmeric

Turmeric is much used in oriental cuisine. It is one of the basic ingredients of curry powder, Thai fish and meat curries and Indian rice dishes. It has an intense, yellow colour, but it should not be confused with saffron which has a very different taste.

### vanilla

The fruit pods (beans) of the tropical vanilla orchid tree add a delicious aroma to cakes, puddings, ice cream, confectionery and so on. In cakes it is best to use vanilla essence (extract) while to make ice-cream and rice pudding, the crushed pod (bean) is added to the hot liquid so that it releases its delicate aroma. Vanilla sugar is made by leaving a pod (bean) in a container of sugar.

### wasabi

Very sharp green radish usually available as a paste or powder. It is used to season sushi and many other Japanese dishes. It is important not to add too much. Wasabi is usually served separately as well so that every one can mix it to the sharpness they like.

### watercress

Watercress grows in the wild but it should not be eaten in case it contains parasites. Cultivated watercress is readily available. This is grown in watercress beds with pure water of the correct temperature running through them. Watercress has a hot, spicy taste and is delicious on its own, on bread and butter, in green salads, in cream soups, in risottos and in potato salad.

## woodruff, sweet

Smelling of new-mown hay, sweet woodruff is only available in May, and it is therefore best-known as the essential ingredient in the aromatic drinks of traditional Maytime celebrations, such as the May wine cup in Germany and May wine punch in the United States. It is delicious in desserts, such as fresh strawberries marinated in woodruff, or wine jelly with fruit and fresh woodruff.

# Index

The recipes in this book have been carefully researched and worked out. However, neither the authors nor the publishers can be held liable for the contents of this book.

**Picture acknowledgments:**
The editors and publishers thank the following for their help in the creation of this book:
ADAM; Birkel; CMA; Deutsche Butter; Deutsches Teigwaren-Institut; Fuchs-Gewürze; Galbani; Informationsgemeinschaft Bananen; Knorr; Koopmans; Langguth; Maggi; Mazola; Meggle; Mondamin; National Sunflower Association; Peter Kölln, Köllnflockenwerke; Thomy Feinkost-Produkte; Uncle Ben's. Impressionen Versand, Wedel: reproduction page 41; Food Archiv, Munich: pages 63, 71

**The authors:**
Anna Thal lives and works in Munich. She is a freelance author of cookery books and an adviser on health matters.

Dagmar Fronius-Gaier, Dipl. Öko-trophologin, is a freelance author in the field of cookery books. She lives and works in Rosenheim.

**The photographers:**
Brigitte Sporrer and Alena Hrbkova met each other while training as photographers in Munich, Germany. After working as assistants to various advertising and food photographers, they now each have their own studios in Munich and Prague respectively.

**The food stylist:**
Hans Gerlach is a skilled cook and architect from Munich, who also works as a freelance food stylist. His clients include print and TV advertising production companies, and he also contributes his skills to cookery books.

# DUMONT monte

*Already published*

ISBN 3-7701-7001-6

ISBN 3-7701-7004-0

ISBN 3-7701-7002-4
(not available in USA and Canada)

**Each title:**
160 pages
100 colour photographs
230 x 280 mm / 9 x 11 inches
hardcover, £ 9.99 / $ 14.95

☞ **Over 100 classic and creative
new recipes**
☞ **Brilliant value – a great gift buy**
☞ **Easy-to-follow methods**
☞ **100 inspirational photographs**

# DUMONT monte *Already published*

ISBN 3-7701-7046-6

ISBN 3-7701-7029-6

ISBN 3-7701-7003-2

**Asparagus**
c. 150 pages
over 100 colour photographs
230 x 280 mm / 9 x 11 inches
hardcover, £ 9.99 / $ 15.95

**Low Fat**
216 pages
over 120 colour photographs
230 x 270 mm / 9 x 11 inches
hardcover, £ 9.99 / $ 17.95

**Tapas**
164 pages
100 colour photographs
230 x 280 mm / 9 x 11 inches
hardcover, £ 9.99 / $ 14.95